Witness for Christ

WITNESS
FOR
CHRIST

by

John F. Crosby

THE WESTMINSTER PRESS

Philadelphia

LIBRARY OF CONGRESS CATALOG CARD No. 65–12520

Published by The Westminster Press ®
Philadelphia, Pennsylvania

PRINTED IN THE UNITED STATES OF AMERICA

To Mom and Dad

Contents

But you shall receive power when the Holy Spirit has come upon you; and you shall be my witnesses in Jerusalem and in all Judea and Samaria and to the end of the earth.—Acts 1:8.

Foreword

THERE IS AN OLD STORY about a pastor who had preached a resounding sermon on Christian service. The sermon emphasized service within the church and beyond the church. At the conclusion of the service, as the pastor was greeting the congregation at the door, a serious-minded gentleman asked the pastor how he could serve. The pastor was surprised, for he wasn't used to such immediate response to his sermons. In addition to his surprise, he was also embarrassed, for he had no ready answer!

The problem to be pointed up is that we are long in diagnosis and short in prescription; we are long in theological doctrine and short on the practical application of this doctrine. From our pulpits we hear that Christ laid down no blueprint for the Christian life. With this there can be no quarrel! Yet, does this justify the silence in both spoken and written material concerning such questions as: How should a Christian live? What does it mean to "follow Christ"? What is a Christian disciple? What does it mean to "witness" for Christ?

Have you ever heard a religious discussion that sounded like this?

QUESTION: What does it mean to be a Christian?
ANSWER: It means to follow Christ!
QUESTION: But what does it mean to follow Christ?

ANSWER: It means to do God's will and Christ's will.

QUESTION: But what is God's will? What is Christ's will?

ANSWER: God's will is that we follow Christ!

All too often, this is the reasoning process of clergyman and layman alike! In the name of Christ we do a complete circumlocution of the central issue of our faith. In reducing our faith to simple, practical answers, we have become vague and indefinite. For fear of becoming too legalistic and too rule-conscious, we have unwittingly gone to the opposite extreme of vague generality!

The following pages have but one purpose. The purpose is to give answer to the question: What does it mean to follow Christ? The answer will be in terms of expanding and clarifying the concept of "Christian witness." Obviously, we are to do God's will, but what does God's will mean for me, today, in terms of my witness as a follower of Christ? In short, what does "commitment" mean? What does commitment require of me? Does commitment demand self-discipline?

The idea for this book has arisen within the daily context of my own ministry as a parish pastor. I found myself talking about the ministry of the laity: I preached on the necessity for lay men and women to witness for Christ. I stressed the theological doctrine of the priesthood of all believers and the ministry of reconciliation of which we are all ambassadors, God making his appeal through us (II Cor. 5:16–21).

Yet what tools have we preachers given the laity? Have we helped them in their witness? Have we given them the proper perspective? Have we given them practical helps and concrete suggestions? If God's men and women are to perform the work of ministry, then it goes without saying that they need to be properly equipped (Eph. 4:12). This book is an attempt to give positive, helpful meaning to the concept of being a witness for Christ.

One Christian leader, who is also a clergyman, recently made the statement: "When a minister tells others of Christ, he goes as a paid salesman. But when a layman goes, he goes as a satisfied customer." The sole purpose of this book is to equip an already satisfied customer so that he may gain confidence and strength in the daily performance of his own ministry. We need more "satisfied customers" who will take seriously the ministry of the laity. It is my prayer that this book will help equip some of the saints (God's men and women) for their ministry.

I have made no attempt to conceal my gratitude to Dietrich Bonhoeffer and Francis Ayres. I do not feel that I have rehashed what these men have said, but rather, I feel that I have simply elaborated on the implications of some of their theological insights. Less obvious, but more important, is the debt I owe to Elton Trueblood, whose writings have captured my imagination since my high school days.

In writing this message about witnessing for Christ, I came to realize what a profound influence the Christian lay people of three congregations had made upon my thinking. It is a tribute to the Christian lay people of Baldwinsville, New York, Battle Creek, Michigan, and Saginaw, Michigan, that I even attempted to write such a book as this.

Without the encouragement of my wife I would not have written this book. Our participation in small yoke-fellow groups convinced us that Christians need some practical guidance in the matter of conducting their witness. In addition to my wife, I would like to thank a fine Christian couple, Jack and Polly Wolfe, who read and reread my manuscript, giving me a layman's point of view. My thanks go also to Jean Rice for her faithful rendering of my longhand.

J. F. C.

I

"Follow Me"

> When we are called to follow Christ, we are
> summoned to an exclusive attachment to His per-
> son.—Dietrich Bonhoeffer.

A QUICK GLANCE at any concordance will serve to illustrate
the predominance of the word "follow" in the vocabulary
of our Lord. The Greek word *akoloutheō* is the translation
of the word Jesus used, which we render "follow."

Many things are involved in this word. To follow means
to go after; it means to submit to the will of the one who
leads; it implies personal obedience; it involves loyalty,
allegiance, and fidelity.

William Barclay points out that the Greek connotation
of the word "follow," in Jesus' day, would be similar to the
military allegiance that soldiers would be required to have
for their commander. In addition, this would be the language of a slave attending his master. It is used in following the thread of an argument or in obeying the law.

One who follows Christ is therefore one who obeys, as
in the military, or as a slave would be obedient to his
master. A follower of Christ would be one who places himself in the service of the person whom he seeks to follow.
Dietrich Bonhoeffer, the German pastor-theologian who
was imprisoned by the Nazis on April 5, 1943, and put
to death on April 9, 1945, said this: "It [to follow
Christ] is nothing else than bondage to Jesus Christ alone,

completely breaking through every programme, every ideal, every set of laws."

To follow Christ is to take the first step of discipleship. Without this initial act there can be no faith, no commitment, no sacrifice. So often we try to explain away this initial response to God's call by saying that Christ didn't really mean what the Bible says. Sometimes we hear Jesus' words explained away or watered down, or made into some complicated intellectual proposition. In Matt. 10:38, Jesus says, "He who does not take his cross and follow me is not worthy of me." In Matt. 16:24: "If any man would come after me, let him deny himself and take up his cross and follow me." These two references speak all too clearly. Jesus does not say, "I would like you to give some serious consideration to a new philosophical system I have invented." Nor does he say, "I would like you to try out a new code of ethics concerning the Fatherhood of God and the brotherhood of man." He does not say, "When you get squared away in your marriage and in your new house and in your new job, I would like you to study my new system of religious truth." Jesus does not approach us as a philosopher, a theologian, a teacher, or as a moralist. He approaches us as the Son of God, the Way, the Truth, and the Life. He does not approach us with some sort of proposition in mind. He gives us no indication of compromise or of a desire to compromise. He bids us to follow him on his terms, not on our terms. This is the thrust of Luke 9:57–62, where Jesus encounters three men. Jesus discourages the first from following him because Jesus evidently feels that this man isn't sufficiently aware of the cost of discipleship. To the second man, Jesus said, "Follow me." This man's answer reveals his desire to procrastinate: "Lord, let me first go and bury my father." Jesus' reply at first seems heartless, but upon closer examination, we realize why Jesus answered the way he did. If the man's father were dead, why was he out here? Was not this second man saying, "I will follow you after my father has died"? This might be five, ten, twenty, fifty years in the future! The third man couldn't break with the past. "I will follow you, Lord; but let me first say farewell to those at my home." This appears to be a very reasonable and legitimate request. Once again it behooves us to study Jesus' attitude in this situation, and to ask why he would be so hard on this man who generously offers his life. We miss the point if we think Jesus is here making an attack on family life. Jesus is much more concerned about the two words, "but first." These are the two words we all use to delay an action or a decision. These are the words which indicate that we are not quite ready. These two words telegraph the speaker's intent, which in this case is to postpone commitment. Jesus' reply is pointed: "No one who puts his hand to the plow and looks back is fit for the kingdom of God." Jesus senses that it is really not this man's family that is drawing him home, as much as it is his hesitation to break with his past.

Consider the rich young ruler (Matt. 19:21). Jesus said to him, "If you would be perfect, go, sell what you possess and give to the poor, and you will have treasure in heaven; and come, follow me." We can conclude from this that Jesus does indeed drive a hard bargain. It is Jesus who lays down the terms and not the rich young ruler. Scripture simply says: "When the young man heard this he went away sorrowful; for he had great possessions" (Matt. 19:22). This young man was at least honest with Jesus; he was not willing to pay this high price; he therefore would refuse Jesus' invitation.

One cannot talk about the subject without recalling the disciple Peter's bold affirmation of faith. "Peter declared to him [Jesus], 'Though they all fall away because of you, I will never fall away.' Jesus said to him, 'Truly, I say to you, this very night, before the cock crows, you will deny me three times.' Peter said to him, 'Even if I must die with you, I will not deny you.' And so said all the disciples." (Matt. 26:33–35.) Peter was the one who first confessed Jesus as the Christ of God. Peter was the "chief" of followers. Yet he fell away! We shall have more to say about the "falling away" process in the last chapter; for now, it is enough to point to the fact that although Peter fell away, he did not fall away permanently. He came back stronger than ever after his humiliating experience of failure.

At this point we must be painstakingly careful to stress the fact that, in order to follow Jesus, we need not have reached a certain level of goodness or piety or religiosity. Jesus calls us to follow him, and this call comes to us at the very point where we work and live and eat and sleep. To follow Jesus is no guarantee that we will not "fall away" as did Peter. It is, however, to say that we accept Christ's call on his terms—not on ours. He writes the ticket; he calls the plays.

Two important thoughts concerning the words "Follow me" remain to be considered. First, in Matt. 19:27, we read: "Then Peter said in reply, 'Lo, we have left everything and followed you. What then shall we have?' " This question is often thought, but is seldom spoken. It is natural that Peter be the one to ask it for us. Jesus' answer is disappointing to those who desire earthly reward. Jesus' answer is intelligible only to those who trust his words concerning eternal life. It is a temptation for all of us who take Jesus seriously to take upon ourselves the martyr's complex, thinking proudly of all that we have forsaken in order to follow Christ. We righteously protest with Peter that we ought to get something in return. In other words, the question, What's in it for me? is always with us. It is not a shameful question, but a very normal question. Jesus took this question seriously by giving an answer that promises us the greatest gift of all, the gift of eternal life. But his answer (Matt. 19:28–30) is not without a solemn warning: "But many that are first will be last, and the last first."

Second, we turn to John 21:22. "Jesus said to him [Peter], 'If it is my will that he [referring to John the disciple whom Jesus loved] remain until I come, what is that to you? Follow me!' " Here we see repeated the familiar words, "Follow me." We often ask, "But what about the South Sea islanders who never heard of Christ or of the Bible? What about the Communists inside China and Russia who have never been touched by the gospel? What about the other religions of the world: Buddhism, Hinduism, Judaism, Taoism, Islam, Confucianism? Is there not a case to be made for these religions? By way of answer, we must say that all religions contain elements of truth and beauty, of justice and love. The basic fact we must cope with is that in the Gospels, Christ meets us and challenges us by asking us to "follow" him. At this point it is as if he tells us not to worry about the Buddhists and Hindus or the South Sea islanders. Here he summons us to mind our own affairs first! "If it is my will that he remain until I come, what is that to you?" Peter was being overly inquisitive. He had transgressed his rightful limit of knowledge. He was eager to know what Jesus was going to do about *someone else!* We can be sure that the concern of Peter was appreciated, just as our concern for the safety, comfort, and welfare of our fellowman is certainly a part of our Christian concern. On the other hand, there are limits to what we can know. What about heaven and hell? What about the devil? What about miracles? The temptation is to postpone our moment of decision until we know all the intellectual answers and alibis, or until we have all our doubts answered. Yet, through it all, Christ still speaks to us and warns us to stick to the fundamentals.

In his moving book about his imprisonment at the hands of the Japanese during World War II, Ernest

Gordon describes how he and his fellow prisoners were faced with doubts, and yet they knew they had to come to a moment of decision. "We were involved too because of our doubts. Many of us had turned to Christianity from unbelief and still carried with us our fear of faith. . . . Our doubts were our inheritance as children of our times. We had two alternatives: we could choose the way of men, based on the sovereignty of the natural order, closed, sealed, and impersonal; or we could choose the way of Jesus Christ, free and personal, based upon the sovereignty of God, the Father. The wind of the Spirit had blown upon us; we could not prove how or whence it had come. But our experience pointed to a source beyond ourselves. We knew personal fulfillment, love, joy, peace, wholeness, *as we committed ourselves to the One who called us.* Only as we *responded* to this Word did we receive the power to progress toward true humanity." (Italics mine.)

As long as we stand at the beginning of a path wondering where it goes, we can only question, debate, or speculate. Our answer comes only as we walk down that path. As we journey down this path, we walk by faith, not by sight. As we proceed on our journey, some of the answers come forth—not all the answers, but enough to sustain our pilgrimage. This call to discipleship begins with *obedience* to the One who calls us. Even the disciples did not know a great deal about Jesus when he called to them, "Follow me and I will make you become fishers of men." Yet the New Testament reports their response: "And immediately they left their nets and followed him" (Mark 1:17–18).

The "call" demands a response. It may be a response of acceptance or of rejection. If the call is to be accepted, then this acceptance requires definite steps of decision and commitment. Helmut Thielicke has said: "There are really only two ways to take a thing seriously. Either you renounce it or you risk everything for it. . . . There is no third choice." To become disciples and witnesses of Jesus Christ involves our willingness to risk everything for him.

What is this "call"? Does God call you but not me? Does he call some and ignore others? For our purpose in describing the "call," we turn to a definition by Francis O. Ayres. "The basic, primary Biblical use of the term 'calling' is an urgent invitation *to enter into a life of service to God, a life of forgiveness, meaning, purpose, and freedom.* It is issued to *all men* without distinctions of any kind. A clergyman, no matter how high his office, has received the call in exactly the same way as everyone else and for exactly the same purpose—to serve God in all areas of his life." (Italics mine.) By this we see that God calls all men, not merely a chosen few. The "call" is an open invitation. If we accept it, we find that he leads us into a community or a fellowship of his followers that is called the "church," the body of Christ. Hence one can never be an "individual Christian." Therefore one cannot divorce himself from the community of believers and still claim to be a follower of Christ. By definition, a Christian is a follower of Christ who willingly consents to being led.

II

The Disciple and Discipline

> The discipline we need is not something which we can learn alone. We become trained and disciplined for service only as we are yoked together. Thus, significantly, it is in Christ's clearest call to personal commitment—that in which He says, 'Come to me'—that He also says, 'Take my yoke upon you.' The Company of Christ is tied together by Christ's yoke. That is why 'yokefellow' is a synonym for committed Christian.—Elton Trueblood.

THE GREEK WORD *mathētēs* is rendered "disciple." A *mathētēs* was a "learner" and so a disciple referred first to a learner, a student, or a pupil. In the New Testament the word "disciple" is used only in the Gospels and The Acts, and it is used more than 255 times. In The Acts, the word "disciple" refers specifically to a follower of Jesus, or those who believed in Christ (Acts 6:1, 2,7; 9:1; 11:26).

In Eph. 6:4, the Revised Standard Version reads: "Fathers, do not provoke your children to anger, but bring them up in the *discipline* and instruction of the Lord" (italics mine). It is significant that here the Greek word *paideia* is rendered "discipline." The King James Version translated the word *paideia* as "nurture," and *The New English Bible* translates it "instruction." Hence: "And, ye fathers, provoke not your children to wrath: but bring them up in the *nurture* and admonition of the Lord" (italics mine). *The New English Bible* translates this verse: "You fathers, again, must not goad your children to resentment, but give them the *instruction,* and the correction, which belong to a Christian upbringing" (italics mine). There is

Here we see a distinct relationship between "disciple" and "discipline." In the English, the connection is obvious: a "disciple" is one who stands under (or submits himself to) a "discipline." In this case, the discipline is the discipline of Christ. Just as figuratively we "stand under" the cross of Christ, so do we "stand under" the resulting discipline of Christ.

The relationship between the disciple and basic Christian discipline is beginning to be rediscovered by the church. Too long have we Christians perpetuated the "free and easy" myth of religion! Too long have we simply echoed Madison Avenue! We have been convinced that it is the "instant" that is good. Instant results! Instant action! Instant flavor! As if this heresy in itself were not detrimental enough, we then have compounded the myth by declaring that there is no price connected with God's love and his redeeming forgiveness. It is little wonder the masses of today's churchgoers have little or no idea of what "commitment" really is, because for so long we have tried to woo modern man into the church and into its self-centered program of spectator religion. No wonder stewardship still is thought of in terms of bazaars, bake sales, rummage sales, peddling, and church dinners! No wonder the preacher who echoes the resounding terms of Christ's call is thought of as being "way out" and a product of an unenlightened seminary!

In its simplest form the theology of the New Testament affirms and reaffirms that we are saved by grace (God's lavish love and unlimited forgiveness) through faith. The good news is that Christ died for us, meaning "in our behalf." The proclamation of the New Testament is that we are all in the same boat and none of us is able to earn God's love or in any way to merit God's forgiving pardon. In this regard, our salvation, or our redemption, is absolutely free. It is completely and utterly free, so that we cannot even pay a small down payment. It is not 90 percent God and 10 percent me. It is not even 99 percent God and 1 percent me. It is 100 percent a free act of a loving God who becomes for us a father and longs for us to accept his free gift and respond to him.

It is at this point that we must seek to understand the meaning of the word "response." For it is our response that now becomes so important in this entire relationship. Our entire faith is a faith "in response." Consider I John 4:10,11: "In this is love, not that we loved God but that he loved us and sent his Son to be the expiation for our sins. Beloved, if God so loved us, we also ought to love one another." Consider Rom. 12:1: "I appeal to you therefore, brethren, by the mercies of God, to present your bodies as a living sacrifice, holy and acceptable to God, which is your spiritual worship." Paul had been setting forth a premise and developing it over the first eleven chapters in Romans. His thesis is that our response is a response of our whole being! That's why he uses the word "body" instead of the more ethereal "spirit"! The author of I John says that our response is to love God in return and to express God's love by loving our fellowman.

A careful reading of the entire New Testament will bring forth fresh insight when we read it in this "response" perspective! "Response out of gratitude" is the foundation stone of all Christian ethics and of all Christian practice.

Now let us ask, "Exactly what does this response entail?" In answering this, we pinpoint the central issue, for it is in our response that we experience the "cost" of our redemption. Again, we can do no better than to reflect on the New Testament. This response requires our very life! In the oft-quoted phrase of Bonhoeffer, "when Christ calls a man He bids him come and die." Jesus called men to follow him until the death! Jesus did not say, "Now, because I have given you forgiveness and new life, you must now go to church three times a week"! He did not say, "Now, because I die for you, you must give 10 percent of your income to the church"! He did not say, "Now, because God loves you and longs for you, you must pray three times a day, work for the church (whatever that means), grit your teeth and 'be nice' to your employer." How many people suffering from some sort of guilt complex have prescribed their own penitence by forcing themselves to work on bake sales, dinners, programs, etc.? They feel that this self-inflicted punishment will "atone" or "make up" for their moral infraction or secret sin; after a due period of chastisement, God and the person will at last be all even!

The only trouble with this is that it is not in the New Testament; it is not in the Gospels or in Paul's letters. What's worse, it is so alien to the message and spirit of Christ that one wonders how we Christians ever "got hold" of such a heresy.

What, then, does this response entail? The response means that we give all that we are to Jesus Christ—all that we were, all that we hope to be, all that we have, all that we have not, all that we desire, all that we have done and will do. Christ asks our hearts, our minds, our wills, our bodies, our emotions, our moods, our feelings, and our sexual drives; he asks for me. This is the only response he is willing to accept. "Love so amazing, so divine, demands my life, my soul, my all." Many of the great hymns of the church do a far better job of proclaiming this fact than do the clergy: Frances Ridley Havergal has expressed clearly what many poets and lyricists have expressed in various words and images.

Take my life and let it be
Consecrated, Lord, to Thee.
Take my moments and my days;
Let them flow in ceaseless praise.

Take my hands, and let them move
At the impulse of Thy love.
Take my feet and let them be
Swift and beautiful for Thee.

Take my voice, and let me sing,
Always, only, for my King.
Take my lips, and let them be
Filled with messages from Thee.

Take my silver and my gold;
Not a mite would I withhold.
Take my intellect, and use
Every power as Thou shalt choose.

Take my will, and make it Thine;
It shall be no longer mine.
Take my heart, it is Thine own;
It shall be Thy royal throne.

Take my love; my Lord, I pour
At Thy feet its treasure store.
Take myself, and I will be
Ever, only, all for Thee.

This is the response, and here it is that we begin to
understand the meaning of Christian discipline. We must
focus our eyes upon an army that has trained and worked
and continues to train and work! We must focus upon a
baseball team that arrives daily at the stadium two and
a half hours before game time. The fine edge of readiness
is of vital importance. We must focus upon the musician
who is to perform; he is in constant practice. We must
focus upon the actor, or upon the golfer. Discipline in this
sense is the key to success! Without discipline there could

be no trophy, no prize, no championship. Remember Paul's words: "Do you not know that in a race all the runners compete, but only one receives the prize? So run that you may obtain it. Every athlete exercises self-control in all things. They do it to receive a perishable wreath, but we an imperishable" (I Cor. 9:24–25).

Discipline requires one indispensable ingredient that is the wellspring of all witness, outreach, love, and service. This ingredient is prayer. Prayer is the voice of faith: it is the lifeline of all Christian living and witness. Christ depended on prayer for his daily sustenance. Can we do less? Discipline begins with prayer, is nourished constantly with prayer, and ends with prayer. Without the daily practice of prayer, it is questionable if any meaningful and enduring discipline will be attained. The entire thesis of discipline is a simple recognition that we do not grow unless we expose ourselves to the sources of our faith. The goal of the Christian is to become mature in Christ. (Eph. 4:11–16; Col. 1:28.) Maturity in Christ cannot be achieved on a diet of church organizational meetings, dinners, dances, or recreational programs. Maturity in Christ can be ours only when we are nourished on constant prayer and meaningful exploration of the Scriptures.

The call to discipleship is a call to serious discipline. This discipline is so rugged that only the "grateful" will manage fidelity in participation! This discipline is so strenuous that it cannot be done alone. It is this fact which renews us in our relationship to the church. Only when we come to experience the church in the depth of genuine Christ-centered fellowship does the church become for us what it was for the early disciples. In the experience of the early disciples, the church was a sharing fellowship. The book of The Acts portrays the early church, not as a building, but as a dynamic fellowship of men and women committed to Jesus Christ.

Here we must pause to consider a word from the New

Testament that is very difficult to translate into meaningful English. The word is *koinōnia*. To the modern ear the
word "fellowship" means a variety of things. Robert Raines
has given a good account of the problem when he says:
"Everybody is having fellowship these days. Service clubs,
sewing circles, poker clubs, churches—all have fellowship.
The word 'fellowship' conveys various meanings to various
people. . . . The great word 'fellowship' is used to describe
so many forms of human association that its meaning has
become degraded into mere gregariousness, of a hail-
fellow-well-met-and-soon-forgot nature. So when we of the
church try to explain what we mean by 'Christian fellowship' we have to qualify and enlarge the term to fit the
experience. We speak of the redemptive fellowship, the
fellowship of the concerned, the fellowship of sharing, car-
ing, and bearing."

Koinonia is the experienced presence of the Holy Spirit
within the fellowship of men and women who have sought
to turn their lives completely over to the rule and guidance
of Jesus Christ. When persons have responded to God's
reconciling work in Christ, they experience a new relationship with their fellow Christians who have similarly responded. This new relationship is a redemptive, life-
sharing experience completely different from the ordinary
kind of "fellowship" we hear about in most churches today.
This discipline within the koinonia is a very cutting thing:
it involves us in corporate worship and in smaller study
or sharing groups. Koinonia means literally "fellowship in
Christ"; it refers to those who have responded to Christ's
call and now seek to live under Christ's discipline.

The disciple, therefore, is one who has responded to
the good news by casting himself utterly and completely
in total self-abandon upon the promises of Jesus Christ.
He is a committed person and the discipline of his daily
commitment is the sustaining force, the life-giving source
of all that he is and does. This discipline is both individual and corporate, never just one or just the other.

III

Witness Beyond Morality

He has showed you, O man, what is good;
and what does the Lord require of you
but to do justice, and to love kindness,
and to walk humbly with your God?
(Micah 6:8)

ONE OF THE MOST TREACHEROUS and deceiving heresies
of the modern age, which seeks to undermine the witness
of the church and the proclamation of the gospel, is the
proposition that "Christianity is equal to and the same
as basic American morality."

There probably will be no end to the person who seeks
to rationalize his own actions by saying: "Well, after all,
I'm a good person. I live by the ethics of Jesus and the
Bible." To this type of mind, "goodness is Christianity"
and "Christianity is goodness." As Robert McAfee Brown
reminds us:

> Most people, whether "religious" or not, would
> agree that it is a good thing to "do justice" and to
> "love kindness" (though they might not agree to
> the walking-humbly-with-God part). "That's what
> we need," they would say, "more justice, more
> kindness."
> But notice that the Biblical view is utterly dif-
> ferent. Justice and kindness are not important
> merely in themselves, even though they are ethical

demands of a high order. They are significant
because they are what God requires of us. It is
because he wills us to do justice and to love kindness that we must take them seriously.

Common morality, however, becomes for many people
the sum and substance of the Christian faith. Space pro-
hibits a thorough treatment of the many forms and subtle-
ties of this heresy, but it is sufficient to say that this line
of reasoning is most frequently used to justify one's lack
of church relationship or one's dead church relationship.
The reasoning is such that Jesus was a "good" man and
that we are to be "good" people. When this is attempted,
there is no need for the church and all the bothersome
associations that are related to "churchiness."

Once this heresy is exposed and recognized for what it
is, i.e., an excuse for the "individual Christian" (a self-
contradictory expression), we can then go on to face the
real issue that morality raises as it relates to our Christian
witness. The thesis of this chapter is that Christian witness is more, much more, than morality. Where Christian
witness is equated with morality and where morality is
considered even as the major factor of Christian witness,
we miss the point.

The question is this: What is the relationship between
morality and the Christian faith? Respectable morals are
a prerequisite in becoming a *witness* for Christ, but morality is not, has not been, and never shall be a *prerequisite*
for becoming a *Christian.* We come here to one of the
timeless truths of Christendom, that Jesus Christ changes
us. He takes us and refashions us. Our past may be neu-
tral. It may be filth-ridden or guilt-ridden. It may have
been very moral or very immoral. Nevertheless, the truth
holds that in Christ we are new creatures: the old self is
no longer! The new self, the new being, the new creation
is the result of his grace. "Behold, I make all things new."
(Rev. 21:5.)

Once the new creation is fashioned, once we are men "in Christ," then we are ready to concern ourselves with our witness-response. It is here that we must see to it that our life and mode of conduct are beyond moral question; for if we are immoral or unethical, then we shall never be able to give effective Christian witness. We must insist, therefore, that morality is a prerequisite to Christian witness. It is not to be identified per se with Christian witness, but it is a necessary prerequisite. It is a precondition that must be met. When Jesus spoke to the woman taken in adultery, he parted with these words: "Go, and sin no more." She could henceforth express her gratitude through her witness-response, which from this point forward must be characterized by wholesome moral conduct.

When we turn to Paul's letters, we find several passages devoted exclusively to the moral manner of life. There is no escape from the fact that "common morality" was not practiced and accepted among the ancient Greeks and Hebrews as we practice it today, if even nominally.

"Finally, brethren, we beseech and exhort you in the Lord Jesus, that as you learned from us how you ought to live and to please God, just as you are doing, you do so more and more. For you know what instructions we gave you through the Lord Jesus. For this is the will of God, your sanctification: that you abstain from immorality; that each one of you know how to take a wife for himself in holiness and honor, not in the passion of lust like heathen who do not know God; that no man transgress, and wrong his brother in this matter, because the Lord is an avenger in all these things, as we solemnly forewarned you. For God has not called us for uncleanness, but in holiness. Therefore whoever disregards this, disregards not man but God, who gives his Holy Spirit to you.

"But concerning love of the brethren you have no need to have any one write to you, for you yourselves have been taught by God to love one another; and indeed you do love all the brethren throughout Macedonia. But we exhort you, brethren, to do so more and more, to aspire to live quietly, to mind your own affairs, and to work with your hands, as we charged you; so that you may command the respect of outsiders, and be dependent on nobody." (I Thess. 4:1–12.)

Notice how Paul says, "This is the will of God. . . : that you abstain from immorality" (v. 3). Then notice how Paul goes beyond morality and says, "We exhort you . . . to aspire to live quietly, to mind your own affairs, and to work with your hands . . . ; *so that* you may command the respect of outsiders" (vs. 10–12).

Without common morality, the Christian will never have an effective witness because he will not command the respect of outsiders. Yet, Paul never appears to stop at this point! Morality is a basic ingredient to effective Christian witness, but Christian witness goes beyond morality. Consider Paul's attitude in the following verses:

"But we beseech you, brethren, to respect those who labor among you and are over you in the Lord and admonish you, and to esteem them very highly in love because of their work. Be at peace among yourselves. And we exhort you, brethren, admonish the idle, encourage the fainthearted, help the weak, be patient with them all. See that none of you repays evil for evil, but always seek to do good to one another and to all." (I Thess. 5:12–15.)

"Do all things without grumbling or questioning, that you may be blameless and innocent, children of God without blemish in the midst of a crooked and perverse generation, among whom you shine as lights in the world." (Phil. 2:14–15.)

" 'All things are lawful for me,' but not all things are helpful. 'All things are lawful for me,' but I will not be enslaved by anything. 'Food is meant for the stomach and the stomach for food'—and God will destroy both one and the other. The body is not meant for immorality, but for the Lord, and the Lord for the body." (I Cor. 6:12–13.)

"Do you not know that your body is a temple of the Holy Spirit within you, which you have from God? You are not your own; you were bought with a price. So glorify God in your body." (I Cor. 6:19–20.)

Numerous passages resembling the above are to be found throughout the New Testament. In all cases we must observe that morality is important, but that other things are involved in Christian witness. As far as Christian ethics are concerned, being good is never enough.

A brief review of the following passages will give us a flavor of the New Testament stance concerning morality and the "beyond morality" areas:

    Ephesians 4:1–3, 17–32; 5:1–2, 4–20; 6:10–17
    Colossians 1:9–12, 21–23, 28–29; 2:6–7, 2:20 to
      3:17; 4:5–6
    I Peter 1:13–16; 2:11–17; 3:15; 4:1–5
    II Peter 1:5–7
    I John 2:6; 3:13–18; 4:7–12, 18–21; 5:1–5
    Titus 2:1–5; 3:1–8

Inevitably this becomes the point at which Protestant Christianity is most misunderstood. The doctrine of justification by grace alone means that we are loved, saved, accepted, forgiven, acquitted by God alone. This is 100 percent an act of God, and man has nothing to do with it except to reject this "grace" or to accept it. Then comes the question: "If God is the one who saves, and if he will forgive and forgive, then why bother to be Christian? Why bother to be good? Why not eat, drink, and be merry? Why not have one fling after another? Why not sow our wild oats? We can always confess and repent on our deathbed!"

The New Testament treats this question in the parable of the prodigal son (Luke 15:11–32), which is really a parable about a loving father's relationship to his two sons.

The elder son was a model of faithful sonship! The younger wanted a taste of life without parental authority. Neither son earned the love of his father, because love, by its very nature, cannot be earned. The father loves his two sons regardless of their morality, regardless of their obedience to their father, regardless of their accomplishments in life. Love cannot be earned! Love cannot be merited. (This is *not* to say that the father wasn't ashamed of his younger son and proud of his elder son.) God's love for mortal man is identical in substance to that of the father of the prodigal. We cannot earn God's love; we cannot merit God's acceptance or his forgiveness. How can we earn a gift that is already freely given?

Thus the question arises: What can we do? What should we do? What is left for us to do? By way of answer, it becomes clear that we can either accept this free gift and *live in response* to it or we can reject it. If we reject it, then we alone are responsible for our decision. But if we accept this gift, we cannot flippantly say, "See—God loves me regardless of what I do, so I'll go ahead and do what I please." The reason we cannot do this is that once we understand the meaning of the gift we have accepted, our entire life becomes changed; for now everything we do and everything we are is a response to God's love for us. Our only mission in life is now so to live that we seek to be worthy recipients of God's great gift. Therefore our entire life becomes a life of grateful response. This is why we are good, clean, upright, decent, and moral! Not because by so doing we earn God's love or earn our reward in heaven, but because we seek to be worthy recipients of God's free gift; we seek to respond to this life-giving gift out of a deep sense of gratitude.

This is the motive of our ethic! This is the motive of our entire Christian discipleship: gratitude to God for his boundless love for us. Because he loves us, we are able to love him in response.

In conclusion, we must again remind ourselves that our Christian witness is our response to what God has done for us through Christ. Through the boundless and limitless love of God we are accepted, we are cleansed, we are forgiven, we are justified. Nothing we do can "earn" or "merit" what God chooses to do for us. We do not earn his love any more than a child earns his parents' love. We do not merit his forgiveness any more than a child can earn his parents' pardon. However, just as in the case of the human family, we can now resolve to live out our lives in response to the love that we already experience and that has been freely given to us. Out of gratitude we seek to be worthy of what has been freely bestowed upon us. We cannot "pay back" our parents for sacrifices and hardships that they endured for us except as we seek to live in response to this love by living a life that seeks to show itself worthy in thought, word, and deed. And so too, although we can never "atone" or "make up" or "pay back" to God, or "make recompense to him" for what he has done for us, we can accept the gift of his love, mercy, and forgiveness, and then choose to dwell within this grace in such a way that we show our gratitude by living our life in response. As it says in I John 4:10–11: "In this is love, not that we loved God but that he loved us and sent his Son to be the expiation for our sins. Beloved, if God so loved us, we also ought to love one another." All we can do is to accept the gift and seek to live as worthy recipients. This is the basis of the Christian ethic:

From God's love . . . . . to our gratitude

From our gratitude . . . . . to our response

From our response . . . . . to our witness

Therefore, in defining more precisely our witness, let us see that it includes a response of joyful morality; but let us also see that it is much more than morality. Indeed, it is our whole manner of life.

IV

Witness Within the Orders

> Here we see not merely particular spheres of life *within* which we are to act, but orders in accordance with which we have to act, because in them, even if only in a fragmentary and indirect way, God's Will meets us. Hence we call them "Divine Orders." Each of these spheres of life, with its "orders," presents itself to us first of all as a definite way of common life, as a form of social organization.—Emil Brunner.

ONE OF THE PRESENT-DAY heresies that threaten the church is the notion that it is a private sanctuary, divorced from the workaday world and the crossroads of everyday life. Many people picture the church as a haven within the world; as a fortress against the realities of life, as a monastery where people find refuge. In contrast to this we find that Jesus had no such concept in mind. "And I tell you, you are Peter, and on this rock I will build my church, and the powers of death shall not prevail against it." (Matt. 16:18.) "Go therefore and make disciples of all nations, baptizing them in the name of the Father and of the Son and of the Holy Spirit." (Matt. 28:19.)

We will have more to say concerning the church and its role in the Christian faith in a later section. Here it is necessary to say that if one is a follower of Christ, a disciple, a servant, an apostle, an ambassador, then it is *im-*

possible to be such without coming to terms with and being incorporated into the church. It is a contradiction in terms to say that one can be an "individual Christian" or that one can be a "private disciple." To be a Christian is precisely to be a part of the living, breathing, working body of Christ, within the orders of life.

When we talk about witnessing within the orders of life, we are referring to the way we conduct ourselves within such specific "orders" as the home, the place of work, the social set, the recreational subgroup, the lodge, the club, the various councils or committees, the political party, or the cultural interest group. It is the firm conviction of the writer that there are three basic major "orders" or "categorical groupings" within the lives of most Christians. These are the family, the place of work, and the church.

THE FAMILY

We need to focus our attention on the Christian's witness within his or her own home. The home is a strange combination of love and freedom. Sometimes love degenerates into bitterness, and freedom degenerates into license. Occasionally we discover that it is sometimes easier to be faithful to one's Christian calling outside the "home" than inside. Sometimes it is easier to love one's enemies than it is to love one's closest friends and associates. At times it is easier to be a faithful witness *away* from one's castle than within.

Nevertheless, if we are to be witnesses and ambassadors for Christ, we must realize that this "discipleship" is equally binding on us *within* the sacred confines of family life as it is without. We serve God here *first*. We are Christ's representatives and ambassadors to our husbands and wives, to our children and relatives, to our neighbors and servants. Basic to our thinking are these questions: Is Christ known through me? Do my children regard me

as a merciless tyrant, or as a loving father who insists on
both discipline and respect? Does my husband see me as
an overworked housewife or as a human spirit in whom
Christ dwells and through whom Christ reveals himself
to others? Does my wife see me as an ordinary husband,
father, and breadwinner, or does she see me as a person
alive in Jesus Christ and alert to the ministry of reconciliation given to us by Christ?

When family discord comes, it is the profane word that
strikes the children's ears, or is it the quiet quest for an
answer through discussion of issues and prayer for guidance? When children insist on their own way and put the
family into a turmoil, is it the love of Jesus Christ that
is reflected in the reaction of the parents, or is it careless
temper tantrums and violent verbal explosions? When
misunderstandings occur between husband and wife, who
prevails? Does the love of Christ pervade our hearts and
minds at this point? When crises come and when bereave-
ment and sorrow strike, is it Christ reflected in our reactions, or is it our own selfishness, self-centeredness, and
resentment?

How do we use our time? Do we do things with the
children that *we* want to do, or things *they* want to do?
Do we spend our leisure time wisely and with purpose,
or do we merely "kill time"? Do we use our time for Christ,
or only and exclusively for self?

How do we use our money? Is it true that people who
call themselves by Christ's name spend far more annually
on amusements, pleasure, and entertainment than they
invest in the Kingdom of God? Is it true that how we
spend our money is an indication of what we believe?
If so, then what kind of witness for Christ do we make
within our own families? How methodically do we save
for Christ? How conscientiously do we teach our children
the ABC's of budget-keeping? How do we teach them to
share their earnings or their allowances with the Lord who

gave us life? How do we spend the portion we keep for our family and personal needs? Is this not a legitimate part of Christian stewardship?

Our witness within the home leads us to family worship. Whether a family calls it "family devotions" or "the family altar" is of little importance. The question of crucial nature is: Do mother and father have personal worship? Do the children pray regularly? Are they taught, shown, led, encouraged, or are they merely talked down to and lectured to and preached to? Is there prayer before meals? Is there a time for sharing experiences and insights? In many so-called "Christian families" it appears that we have ushered the Lord of Life right out the back door of our homes.

Yet, we dare not idolize the family! We dare not make children, husband, wife, or loved ones into false gods! This is a very subtle temptation, and one that gets more of a hold on us than we care to think. Our ultimate trust and our first trust must be God in Jesus Christ. Mortal flesh will never be able to support us or give our lives ultimate purpose.

One final word needs to be said concerning the family: If Dad is "at the church" five nights a week, and if nine out of every ten pies are carried off to the church for a bake sale or a church supper, and church activities and programs dominate our lives in an unbalanced proportion, then something is wrong! Is it the task of the church to *undermine* the home? Is it the purpose of the church to make us into church-centered families or Christ-centered families? The family must allow time for the work of the church; the church must allow time for the family. The family and the church should not infringe on each other.

THE PLACE OF WORK

The second area or "order" wherein we do the will of God is in our place of work. For some, this may be the shop, the factory, the plant, the store, the office, or on the road selling. For others, it will involve a profession; for still others, it will be in the home and will concern itself with the management of domestic affairs. There are the "entangling alliances" connected with the role of housewife, mother, parent, taxi driver, volunteer worker, etc.

It should be apparent to us that life is structured so that work is part and parcel of the meaning of life. Biblical support at this point is overwhelming. Paul worked. Christ worked. We work. Without work we would decay! Work is a window through which the divine light shines in a most peculiar way.

How we do our daily work is vitally important! If the work we are given to do is not done well, the thrust of our total Christian witness is lost. Without getting into the whole area of Christian vocations and the different kinds and types of work a Christian ought to do, let it be said that unless a person becomes a witness for Christ in the very place in which he finds himself, he is evading his Christian responsibility. Where do we find ourselves? Some of us find ourselves working on railroad ties or telephone wires, some over hot stoves or noisy typewriters. The point to be made is that we do not postpone our witness until we "get a more Christian job" or "until we get promoted" or "until we get that new account." In the act of postponing, we are putting off Christ. We are saying "not yet" to him who calls us.

It is at this point that we encounter another tragic heresy of our modern day. This heresy is the one that considers the ministry as *the* full-time Christian vocation. To speak of "Christian" work means, according to this line of thinking, that only those people who in one way or another are employed by the church or a related institution are really engaged in "full-time Christian service." This is heresy! This "service" is no more a part-time job for the Christian who is a tool and die worker than it is a part-time job for the clergyman. *According to the New Testament, Christianity is "full-time" for all who call themselves by Christ's name.* If we want to refer to those employed by the church as being in "full-time *church* work," there would be no quarrel, and our terminology would be far better.

Volumes have been written concerning the Christian and his "vocation." Some people talk about "Christian jobs" and others speak about being called to be a lawyer or a salesman. We must note that some jobs or vocations lend themselves to the concept of service to humanity much better than others. Yet our technological society demands that we have production-line workers, shift workers, maintenance men, and efficiency experts. How are these men and women to "witness" while on the job? The only relevant answer to this question in today's technological framework is simply to say that one witnesses primarily in the way he does his designated task and in the way he relates to his co-workers, his supervisors, and to those whom he supervises. Christ is concerned with people. Most jobs expose us to people, for whom Christ lived and died. Therefore our witness is in the relationship we have with these people. Howard Clark Kee says that we must "seek for *opportunities naturally associated* with the work through which a sense of fulfillment may be gained." The opportunities are numerous if we are alert to them. Each situation is a challenge that we must seek to meet wisely, effectively, and creatively.

THE CHURCH

The third area or "order" wherein we do the will of God is through the body of Christ, the church. The brick structure at the corner of Spruce and Main Streets, to which we refer as "our church," is a very important factor in the total perspective of the Christian's witness.

If we define our witness as doing the will of God within

the several orders of our structured lives, then we must see that the church is a very real part in carrying out this witness.

It is a healthy sign to see the church today questioning some of its institutional status. Too often the elaborate administrative structure of the church with its education and music departments has involved Christians in book-keeping, clerical, secretarial, and housekeeping chores to the exclusion of nurture within the koinonia, the fellow-ship in Christ. Therefore, when we talk about the church being the third major "order" wherein we do God's will, we are referring to our *shared life* within the fellowship of Christ.

The church is the Christian's home, his school, his test-ing ground, his proving ground, his learning ground. The faith becomes real to us only as we know the One in whom we put our trust, as we seek to witness to him, and to become his unapologetic followers. Here we are compelled to acknowledge the administrative nature of the institu-tion. A minimum of administration is essential in order that we do a better job with our primary responsibility. Our primary responsibility is to proclaim the Lordship of Jesus Christ over all areas and orders of life.

The church exists as a living fellowship of Christ's disciples who find strength when they gather in his name. The church is not primarily an institution; it is primarily a fellowship of Christ's men and women. As such, it does many things: it exists to preach and to teach, to serve and to witness. The church is a product of our present age and yet it stands above all ages!

We witness to each other *within* the church just as surely as we witness to those *outside* the church. We labor *in* the church and we labor *through* the church. We do *not* identify "churchiness" with the Christian life, but we do recognize that without the institutional church, Chris-tianity is but one generation away from extinction.

A person who thinks he can be a Christian without having anything to do with the body of Christ is simply deluding himself. Christ leads us into the living fellowship of those who have responded to his call. It is true that there are people who live by the Golden Rule and the so-called "principles of Christ," but this amounts to nothing more than the basic morality we discussed in Chapter III. A Christian is one who follows Christ; he gives himself to Christ; Christ becomes the Lord and Master of all personal habits; Christ leads us into the physical presence of others who have similarly responded to his call.

Our witness cannot be confined to the church walls, but it must begin there. Within these walls our faith must be nourished and strengthened, nurtured and deepened. We dare not let the church ever become for us a retreat house or a monastery. It is, rather, a fortress where men and women are groomed for battle and prepared for the consequences thereof. It is a place from which we are sent forth as witnesses and ambassadors, and then as in a war patrol, it is a place to which we return for new strength, renewed enthusiasm, and new armor. When the church is absorbed in its own life to an excessive degree, then it has missed its primary objective.

V

Witness in Thinking, Listening, and Acting

Some people may say that there should be no preaching, but that deeds of love alone should carry their own message. Others will say that only preaching can really tell what God has done, and everything else should be kept secondary or omitted. But it is better to recognize that God has made us with both mouths and hands, both minds and bodies, and all his gifts are meant to be used in sharing his love. The spoken word and the practical deed should reinforce each other, not oppose each other.—Charles W. Forman.

THINKING

THE LIFE OF a Christian begins in the very guarded and secret domain of the mind. Here there is only God and me. Here is the birthplace of my witness. Here is where the greatest issues of my life are decided. Nothing I ever do will receive the go-ahead signal unless it is first given here. All my words, deeds, actions, reactions, and habits will be sent out from this headquarters: my witness begins with the way I think.

This area of our witness determines all other areas. Here hypocrisy is either abhorred or approved; here sincerity is or is not. Here a man's true colors are shown: he can either live with himself or seek to escape from himself. Here a man's conscience is either bent toward God or toward greed and self-satisfaction. Here the true motive is shown, both to God and to oneself.

Our whole attitude toward life, toward others, toward ourself; our attitude toward our employer, our employees, our fellow workers, our competitors; our attitude toward our client, toward our account, toward our patient, toward our customer, toward our "prospect"—all this is part of our mind's witness.

What thoughts do we actually think when we make a sale? What thoughts go through our mind when we answer a client's questions or objections? What do we *really* think of our competitor or our employer or our patient?

What do we really think about our husband or our wife or our in-laws? What do we really think about our parents, our neighbors, our neighbors' children, or our own children?

It has been well said that life as we know it would be impossible if others could read our thoughts. The Creator certainly was wise in creating us to have this one area of privacy, and it is interesting to note that the illnesses we describe today as mental often stem from our own embarrassment, guilt, and shame over the thoughts of our minds!

This leads us to the fact that our witness begins in our own mind. What is my personal, private witness that I choose to make to God? What is my witness to myself? What do I believe about life and God? Why? What does this mean for me? What do I hold precious? What do I value? What really counts? Can I respect myself? Do I see myself as bearing the impression of God's image? How can I most faithfully relate myself to those with whom I have to do? Am I really myself or do I wear a series of masks or false fronts? Who is the real me?

These are hard questions. Introspection of any description is difficult because it is subjective in nature and it is an open question as to when we are being "truly honest" in the process. How much is truth and how much is rationalization or self-justification? This is why true introspection for the purpose of determining our mind's witness is best done in the context of prayer. Without prayer and its ensuing strength, forgiveness, cleansing, and power, we would be helpless to change our inner witness. The truth about ourselves would be unbearable apart from the grace of God's love, which accepts us in spite of our unworthiness. The prayer of confession is absolutely fundamental to the sensitive Christian who takes seriously his day-by-day inner witness. After the confession we should turn to intercession, where we hold those of special need up to God's unsearchable love.

Following our daily prayer, we do well to focus our thoughts on the needs of the day, on the special problems and relationships in such a way that the God-inspired witness of our mind can be translated into the God-inspired witness of word and action.

LISTENING

A second category of our Christian witness is in listening to others. Without careful attentiveness to the words and expressions of others, our witness will probably be irrelevant and ineffective. It will miss the mark.

Listening is the cornerstone of counseling. The pastor, the psychologist, the child-guidance counselor, the psychiatrist, the social worker, and the personnel director all depend on their ability to concentrate on what people say to them. Perhaps our greatest error in witnessing is to assume that we are listening, when in fact we are impatiently waiting to get a word in. Notice how easy it is to "tune" someone out. When children tune out their adult guardians it is usually quite obvious. But we adults have learned to be subtle. We continue to pretend that we are listening, yet in fact we are only hearing words. We look at the person who is speaking, but the thoughts of our mind are on some far distant horizon. We make a pretense at listening, but too often our thoughts are upon what *we* want to say.

There can be no substitute for alert concentration. This is a task for our mind. It requires patience, understanding, and a willingness to allow the other person to reveal himself. Words, sighs, gestures, and facial expressions all contribute to the listening process. Words tell a lot, but the way the words are spoken sometimes tells us much more.

In meeting the needs of people, the witness for Christ must understand that as a listener he is being used by God. Talking can be a catharsis or a healing force if the talking is done in the presence of one who is trusted and respected. A good listener seeks to establish an identification of empathy, which is a "feeling into" the situation of the speaker. It is not easy to enter into the inner emotional experiences of others. Yet we must attempt to do so if we are to be listening witnesses.

John Sutherland Bonnell says in his book *Psychology for Pastor and People:* "Few experiences give the individual more reassurance than to find someone who will listen sympathetically and intelligently to a recital of his difficulties. . . . Telling one's problems to another person clarifies the thought of the troubled individual so that even as he talks he begins to see other facets of the difficulty. Light begins to break upon him."

As witnesses we listen to troubled people and to casual conversation. We listen to cries of despair and to remarks of cynicism. We listen to small talk and we listen to honest, searching questions. We listen to complaints and we listen to accounts of people who are experiencing the joy of exciting personal discoveries.

> The first service that one owes to others in the fellowship consists in listening to them. Just as love to God begins with listening to His Word, so

the beginning of love for the brethren is learning to listen to them. It is God's love for us that He not only gives us His Word but also lends us His ear. So it is His work that we do for our brother when we learn to listen to him. (Dietrich Bonhoeffer.)

ACTING

A third category of our Christian witness is in what we do! We weaken and destroy our witness when we allow the things we do to cancel out the things we say. As the old maxim has it: "I can't hear what you're saying because of what you are." We all know people who talk a good game, who speak freely of Christ, of redemption, of the gospel, and of the things concerning the faith—yet whose witness of action, deed, and character is the diametrical opposite of this witness in word.

In one sense, of course, we are all hypocrites. If we define a hypocrite as a person whose actions do not measure up to his beliefs, then we are guilty of hypocrisy, for who among us except Christ ever lived up fully to what he believed? In this regard, we do well to understand that hypocrisy is an absolute requirement of the Christian faith, for we must be ready to confess that we have fallen far short of our goal. If we define Christianity as "following Christ" or "following in the way," then we must realize that we never actually "arrive." We are always "en route," "on the way," "in the process of becoming."

Thus the question before us is, How ought we to act? First, the Christian needs to learn to be consistent. He must recognize that his Christian witness is never something that can be turned on or off as we do a water faucet, or as we see some people turn charm on and off. Second, the Christian must see his actions not just as deeds. The witness of a Christian is not that of a "good deed done once or twice daily" type of thing. Our witness is a witness of attitude, of action, and of reaction. Our witness means

fighting for certain causes; it means having the right enemies in life. Part of our responsibility as witnesses is in
treating our employees, co-workers, customers, clients, and
competitors as people instead of "things" to be dealt with
or manipulated.

The old criticism about Christians living with split per-
sonalities, one for Sunday and the other for weekdays, is
more often an excuse or an alibi on the part of the person
using it in order to justify himself in staying apart from
both the church and the Christian life. On the other hand,
it is here that we must be on guard lest we fall prey to
the temptation to divide or separate our religion from our
life. The double standard is very appealing to all of us at
times—one standard for me and another for you; one
standard now and another standard later. It is a very subtle
temptation to check our faith at the hat rack before we
begin a day's work or before we negotiate a union-management agreement.

It is a constant temptation to identify our Christian witness with some sort of crusade for a good cause. Our witness at times may call for such a crusade, or campaign,
or rally, or protest; yet we dare not say that this is the
sum and substance of a Christian witness.

We are products of a culture that puts a premium on
"doing" and on "causes" and "campaigns." The danger is
that the positive action, energy, cause, work, and sacrifice
of the "doing" will become a *substitute* for the ongoing
daily witness. We are so action-conscious that we think,
eat, and sleep committees and programs. This is not to say
that these are wrong, but we must be aware that too often
they become an easy substitute for Christian witness
through action on the personal and interpersonal level.
We are living in a day when the church needs desperately
to live out its collective and individual witness in a forth-
right and positive way, with as little fanfare and trumpet-
blowing as possible.

Regarding our "witness through acting," it is well for

us to be aware of another danger. Service within the church, in the form of support to the local church program, while *absolutely essential* to the life of the institutional church, is but *one* part of the comprehensive "witness through action" that we make as followers of Christ. For too many years we have deluded ourselves by making the word "witness" synonymous with "service to the church."

It is in this sense that we are called not to lead "church-centered lives" but "Christ-centered lives." We have already seen that a Christ-centered life involves one in the life and work and worship of the koinonia or "fellowship," but this "involved one" must then sally forth into the world and into contact with people. It is precisely on this issue that the church and the clergy have been criticized so severely in recent years. The criticism, for the most part, is justified because for too long the church has accepted "service through involvement in the church's program" as being equivalent to "the Christian's witness" or to "fulfillment of one's Christian responsibility." On the contrary, God's will may at times be better done by divesting oneself of the barnacles of ecclesiastical machinery and institutional program involvement. This is *not* to be interpreted as justification for leaving the church or for severing ties. It means that we spend too much time in reports, in listening to speakers talk about anything that will draw a crowd, in church supper after church supper. It means that we have become prisoners of the organized program of the institution; too often the koinonia is nowhere to be seen. We need more time and freedom to "minister" creatively to our neighbors, enemies, employers, and employees. The church building and its program can become, and in fact has become for all too many, an easy escape from the sharp-cutting responsibilities we have as Christ's disciples and witnesses to go into all the world making disciples of all nations.

VI

Witness in Speaking

It is one thing to recognize that there is no vital Christianity without witness; it is another to know how a valid witness is to be made. . . . We can begin our answer by observing that testimony must be in both deed and word. The spoken word is never really effective unless it is backed up by a life, but it is also true that the living deed is never adequate without the support which the spoken word can provide. This is because no life is ever good enough. The person who says naïvely, "I don't need to preach; I just let my life speak," is insufferably self-righteous. What one among us is so good that he can let his life speak and leave it at that?—Elton Trueblood.

WHEN WE HEAR a preacher or theologian challenge us to become "witnesses for Christ" we usually get our defenses set, for we certainly have no intention of being door-to-door witnesses like the Jehovah's Witnesses of the Watchtower Society. How easy it is to tell ourselves, "I will witness silently; I will witness through kindly deeds; but I will *never* talk to others about faith or religion."

As has been hinted at in these pages, there is much verbal witness that is a sham, is done in poor taste and with little feeling of genuine love. However, there is a point at which we Christians must speak forth. There is a time for the right word well spoken.

More often than not, the words will come to us when we have devoted sufficient energy to the task of listening. (The promise of Jesus to his disciples holds true for us: "When they deliver you up, do not be anxious how you are to speak or what you are to say; for what you are to say will be given to you in that hour; for it is not you who speak, but the Spirit of your Father speaking through you" [Matt. 10:19–20].)

We are not to be obnoxious in our speaking, nor are we to be overbearing. We are not to be like a phonograph record that keeps playing over and over again. The words we speak we must choose with great care and skill. As Paul says to the Colossians: "Conduct yourselves wisely toward outsiders, making the most of the time. Let your speech always be gracious, seasoned with salt, so that you may know how you ought to answer every one." (Col. 4:5–6.) On the other hand, how many of us would be hard pressed if we were put to the test of declaring the basis of our faith and the nature of the Christian hope in a few words? "Always be prepared to make a defense to any one who calls you to account for the hope that is in you, yet do it with gentleness and reverence." (I Peter 3:15.)

Are we afraid to speak about our faith? Are we reticent to use certain words? Is it not true that when we do speak of our faith to outsiders (or to fellow insiders) we are reluctant to use such words as "God," "Christ," "Jesus," "resurrection," "reconciled"? A remark was once passed to a clergyman after an official board meeting one night, "Why are we afraid to talk about Christ?"

Before we consider this topic any further, let us admit squarely and forthrightly that we are subconsciously fighting the extremes of the fundamentalist groups. They use the buttonhole technique of cornering an innocent by-stander and badgering him with an array of questions that are quite meaningless aside from prior contact and mutual understanding. There are churches and Christian organizations that use this approach with much supposed success. For our purpose we need to be reassured that this is *not* what we mean by "witness through words." We must not yield to the temptation to drop "witness in words" because of the bad connotation a small minority has given it.

If, as we believe, Christ is in us constantly through his Holy Spirit, and if we believe with Paul that "it is no longer I who live, but Christ who lives in me" (Gal. 2:20), then speaking calmly and naturally about this Christ and the meaning to us of his life, death, and resurrection should be as natural as breathing. The connotation becomes unpleasant when we think our speaking should be artificial or affected or forced. We rebel when we are presented with a picture of the superior, enlightened, redeemed Christian forcing his religion down the throat of a poor, ignorant, unregenerate, half-clad heathen. We rebel because this has overtones of a self-righteous, condescending type of Christian love (which is neither truly love nor truly Christian).

In I Peter 3:15, it says that we should be prepared to give account for the hope that is in us with "gentleness and reverence." When, therefore, our verbal witness is anything other than kind and considerate, we fail just as much as if we had said nothing. What could be more natural and wonderful than for the Christian to pass on to someone else what he has himself experienced? Again, this is not the sort of thing that can be rehearsed at home in front of a mirror. You can think about what you might want to say, but you can't actually read off a prepared statement as a politician does to the press. The reason for this is that our witness is valid and vital and alive only as it is a part of a given situation. It is the time, situation, and circumstances that will determine what you say and in what manner.

Sometimes we speak out because we are in a situation where no one has touched on the real reason for an action or a decision; under these circumstances, we feel "constrained" to speak forth because no one else has spoken. A situation of this type could be a political ward meeting, a labor union meeting, or a church circle meeting. Or it could range from a bull session on the Common Market to a bull session on admitting Red China to the United Nations.

Sometimes our witness is from an individual to a group, sometimes from group to group, from a group to an individual (Alcoholics Anonymous), or most frequently, from an individual to an individual.

Is it blasphemous to suggest that witness through words is an art? It is something that we can learn through practice. We work at it; we do not avoid it; we welcome it. We seek to learn the art of tact and gracefulness. We learn to speak in plain language but with a degree of subtleness. When Jesus said we must be "wise as serpents and innocent as doves," he must have been thinking of our words as well as our deeds and our decisions!

Let the reader beware at this point lest he say to himself: "I'll do the other kinds of witnessing, but this verbal type is not my cup of tea. I'll leave it to others better qualified." Who is better qualified? Do you believe in Christ? Have you given him your life? Have you cast yourself upon him so that he shares your burdens and you share his yoke? Do you live daily "in him"? If so, no one is qualified if you aren't. And if you aren't qualified, no one is! Not even Pastor Jones or Father O'Malley or Brother Vernon! Not even Martin Luther or John Calvin or John Knox; not even Augustine or Thomas Aquinas or Francis of Assisi!

We should recall the Old Testament episode when "Moses said to the Lord, 'Oh, my Lord, I am not eloquent, either heretofore or since thou hast spoken to thy servant; but I am slow of speech and of tongue.' Then the Lord said to him, 'Who has made man's mouth? Who makes him dumb, or deaf, or seeing, or blind? Is it not I, the Lord? Now therefore go, and I will be with your mouth and teach you what you shall speak' " (Ex. 4:10–12).

Knowing what to say, when to say it, and how to say it are things that can be learned by any person who is a new creature in Christ. Neither education nor the lack of it can be used as an excuse, nor can shyness and natural reticence be employed as excuse or alibi.

There is nothing more moving or more powerful than the sincere account of how one individual came to the truth about himself, about life, and about God. If we call this account a "testimonial," we become suspicious; we do not want to be identified in any way with anything that resembles self-righteous doting. Although this approach was perhaps good enough for Grandma, and therefore supposedly good enough for me, this doesn't mean that it has to be packaged in the same old can or carton or wrapping paper.

The very words "witness" and "testimony" come from the courtroom. A witness testifies to what he has experienced or to what he has seen or heard. In a very real sense, we are all on trial every day of our lives. As Christians we are judged daily by those all around us: our family, neighbors, friends, co-workers, and our competitors (Christian and non-Christian). A lot of this "judging" is unconscious and covert in nature, but nevertheless it is very real.

If we are on trial, then this places us in the role of the witness who must give account (testimony) of his beliefs and actions. We need to learn to speak about ourselves, our God, and our relationship to him. We must seek to give this account in a positive, wholesome, helpful, and creative way. In giving this testimony we must not be presumptuous, obnoxious, or belligerent! We must not give the feeling of "I'm saved. . . . Too bad you're not," or "You poor, poor person! I'll pray for you."

Words spoken are most frequently spoken in terms of

response. As Christian witnesses we must be alert for our opportunity. We must speak with calculation of the situation and of the mood of our listener.

Life brings to us situations where there is an element of anger and belligerence. Sometimes we find ourselves involved in hostility. Here we must carefully plan our maneuvers. At times we must reply in righteous indignation when the sacredness of human dignity is violated. Jesus himself was reported to have become angry when he looked upon social injustices and when he encountered the money changers who were desecrating the Temple. There are times when we must repel this feeling of anger, and in a soft-spoken voice ask a penetrating question that will cause the listener to stop and think. Sometimes we need to give assurance that we love somone in spite of the hostility of the particular situation.

There are instances when our spoken witness is in response to someone's loneliness or despair. This can be a most crucial time for friendship, but especially for Christlike friendship. Depression is one of the most common human characteristics. The love of a concerned friend is sometimes felt, but often this is simply not enough. Words can lift a person out of the depths of depression, providing these words are spoken from the heart and with a sense of sharing the other's burden.

Our reaction to gossip, rumor, and hatred is of crucial significance. How do we listen to obscene jokes? How do we respond when we hear someone's character being torn to shreds? How do we speak when we are encouraged to condone things that we consider to be ill-suited for Christians?

The list of possibilities for opportunity to witness is limited only by our inability (or our unwillingness) to be open and receptive to the needs and the attitudes of our fellow human beings. These are the people whom Jesus loved. Jesus Christ now seeks to be at home in them through you.

VII

Exercises in Verbal Witness

"But in order that it may spread no further among the people, let us warn them to speak no more to any one in this name." So they called them and charged them not to speak or teach at all in the name of Jesus. But Peter and John answered them, "Whether it is right in the sight of God to listen to you rather than to God, you must judge; for we cannot but speak of what we have seen and heard." (Acts 4:17–20.)

ALTHOUGH PLACE and time alter the circumstances of the individual situation in which we witness, the message to which we witness remains unchanged. We are not eye-witnesses like Peter and John, but we are Christ's men and women who have come to recognize his claim on our lives. Therefore we too cannot but speak of what we have discovered to be the light of our life. But how do we speak? How do we learn to discuss these vital matters with others? Let's look at some examples that may give us some helpful clues.

PROBLEM No. 1

I am a Christian pastor. Our local congregation completed a building fund campaign, and now an educational wing is being built. I was inspecting the job the other day when I overheard this conversation between a concrete-mixing company worker and a bricklayer.

CONCRETE MAN: "Boy, these churches sure must be rich! Probably preach the fear of hell in order to get the suckers to cough up 10 percent."

BRICKLAYER: "Perhaps, but I doubt it! Probably just a group of people pulling together for something they believe in. I know that's the way it is in my church."

CONCRETE MAN: "You belong to this church?"

BRICKLAYER: "No, but we believe pretty much the same things."

CONCRETE MAN: "I still don't see it! If God loves us like they say, then why would he expect people to give up so much to build these churches?"

BRICKLAYER: "I used to feel that way until I had a kidney operation three years ago. When I was flat I began to do some real thinking, and it was then I realized that all I am is due to God's creative power—that without him I would have nothing and I would be nothing, for it is God who gives me bodily strength and energy and health to lay these bricks."

CONCRETE MAN: "Gee, you mean you give money to your church willingly?"

BRICKLAYER: "Yes. It's one of the ways I can say 'thank you, God' for all he has done for me."

CONCRETE MAN: "I'll be damned if I'd ever do that!"

BRICKLAYER: "You may surprise yourself someday!"

The bricklayer handled himself well. He was natural! He was not gooey or sentimental or affected or artificial. He was not presumptuous, obnoxious, or belligerent. He did not take on a condescending, "I'm saved—too bad you're not!" attitude. He was himself and he gave a personal defense of the church and of his hope and faith.

PROBLEM No. 2

I am a housewife living in a moderate-income, average-American suburb. I am a Christian. I have many neighbors and friends who are "nothing." Also, some of my closest friends are members of the church, but rarely attend services. One day I had several of the girls over to my house for midmorning coffee. We got on the subject of the new church being organized in our community.

MRS. HOSTESS: "Why are they starting a new church out here? The city churches aren't that crowded!"

MRS. NOTHING: "Oh, you know these churches—they follow the schools and shopping plazas because they figure this increases their own business."

MRS. BACKSLIDER: "Oh, I didn't know they were organizing a new church out here! Maybe some of these children can learn a little religion. Goodness knows *they* need it!"

MRS. NOTHING: "Yes, but religion won't help. It's not what people believe that matters, it's how they live. As far as I'm concerned, this church business is sheer hypocrisy. If you ask me, these church people ought to put up or shut up."

MRS. HOSTESS: "Well, I can't speak for others, but that's exactly why *I* am a Christian—because my actions do not measure up to my beliefs—because I'm painfully aware of my faults and need help to overcome them."

MRS. BACKSLIDER: "Now, girls, you're both going to extremes. One of you is a nothing and one is a fanatic. Now take me for instance: I belong to the church, but I don't let it interfere with my life!"

MRS. NOTHING: "That's just my point—so why be a hypocrite—why belong?"

MRS. HOSTESS: "I agree with Mrs. Nothing on that— if it isn't going to have any effect on your life, then it isn't worth bothering with. But on the other hand, if one views his or her faith like the electric light circuit that lights up the whole house, then this faith becomes not just another 'part' of life, but the circuit that gives meaning and light to everything else."

MRS. BACKSLIDER: "I still can't see getting all worked up about it."

MRS. NOTHING: "Well, my husband says . . ."

Mrs. Hostess won no victory, but she handled herself well under the circumstances. Obviously, she has her finger on basic realities. Yet, we all must see that the better informed we are about our faith and the more familiar our Bible is to us, the more natural will be our own witness. The value in Mrs. Hostess' approach is to be realized only if her comments made in love and sincerity will somehow penetrate the minds of Mrs. Nothing and Mrs. Backslider, so that at a later time and under different circumstances these thoughts will come to the fore.

PROBLEM No. 3

This problem concerns a fairweather would-be Christian who has a greater loyalty to his bowling team than to his church. He works six days a week and is under normal business pressures by present-day standards.

MR. FAIRWEATHER: "Me—go to church! Look, I believe in God, but not all this church business! This is my only day to rest and sleep and to play golf and bowl. Oh, yes, I'm supposed to keep the house and yard in shape too! Church—for me? No, thanks—I just don't have the time."

MR. INNOCENT (*fellow church member doing church visitation*): "I understand fully your position. I never used to go to church. I always told the pastor, 'I can pray just as well on the golf course or while out fishing or walking in the woods as I can in church with a bunch of stuffed shirts.' The pastor did not argue with me, he just said, 'But do you?' When I became honest with myself I had to admit that church was a means of disciplining myself."

MR. FAIRWEATHER: "Yes, but time is something I don't have."

MR. INNOCENT: "One hour a week in church worship leaves 167 hours for everything else."

MR. FAIRWEATHER: "Sure, but look at what that one hour does to my day! Besides, I can love God and serve him in other ways besides church."

MR. INNOCENT: "I couldn't agree with you more. I know I find it hardest to practice Christ's teachings in my business. People seem to take advantage of you as soon as you try to be a nice guy to them."

MR. FAIRWEATHER: "That's why my motto is 'business first.' The preacher ought to come down to earth with me in my daily routine. He'd sure change his tune!"

MR. INNOCENT: "Perhaps he would—although Pastor Harrison seems to have been around."

MR. FAIRWEATHER: "I still say that I just don't have enough time. Church is O.K. for women, children, and forty-hour-week men, but we are living in the twentieth century, and times have changed."

MR. INNOCENT: "I feel that this decision is yours to make, but I honestly think that perhaps we at the church have let you down because we have failed to help you to see that your relationship to God is the single most important thing in your life."

MR. FAIRWEATHER: "But is there anything wrong with having one's own private religion like I do? After all, I'm a Christian too!"

MR. INNOCENT: "It depends on our definition of a Christian. If a Christian is a follower of Christ, then that means he follows Christ's teaching, his precepts, his example; and if we take him seriously, he eventually leads us even to share his cross and to be a part of his living, active earthly body, his church. It would be difficult to be a follower of Christ without having anything to do with his body, the church."

MR. FAIRWEATHER: "But I don't see why being a Christian means having no fun. I hate to think of giving up bowling and golf."

MR. INNOCENT: "I'm not much of a bowler, but I do like golf, and yet I haven't given up my golf game."

MR. FAIRWEATHER: "I understand that new preacher actually thinks people ought to tithe!"

We have all had encounters like the above. It requires little comment except to say that no matter how well Mr. Innocent answered a question, Mr. Fairweather would hop to another putting green by asking another question, or by passing off a leading remark. Actually this discussion could go on for hours because Mr. Fairweather really doesn't care, and nothing Mr. Innocent says is going to change him. For the person who is used to such jousting, it becomes obvious that to the people who don't *want* to be shown, there is no right answer. Just as soon as any answer comes forth, the question is changed or the ground is shifted. There is no victory!

It should be said that Mr. Innocent handled himself admirably. He didn't fly off the handle, he refrained from condemnation and sarcasm, he didn't get himself into any corners from whence retreat was impossible. He had good answers and they were *his own*.

PROBLEM No. 4

Here we are concerned with an informal social gathering, most of the people being interested, loyal, and active members of the same church. The conversation has gone the rounds and is now focused on the all-too-usual habit of criticizing and petty fault-finding.

MR. UNHAPPY: "I've been a member of the church for thirteen years, but I'm fed up! Nothing is done the way it used to be done."

MRS. HAPPY: "What on earth are you referring to?"

MR. UNHAPPY: "We don't have as many suppers, big socials, or those big money-raising affairs like we used to have. All we do is study and pretend to be religious."

MR. WORN-OUT ORGANIZATION MAN: "Thank God! At last the church can be the church and stop trying to be a social organization and a part-time restaurant."

MR. UNHAPPY: "Then what is the sense in having the church?"

MR. WORN-OUT ORGANIZATION MAN: "The church is primarily a fellowship of those who follow Christ. Its primary function is to help its members grow in this pilgrimage."

MRS. HAPPY: "The church has changed! When I was a girl we had rummage sales, dinners, social programs. But these functions are not needed now because of our changing cultural patterns. I think the church has changed for the best!"

MRS. CONCLUSION-JUMPER: "But why should the church oppose having fun and good fellowship?"

MRS. HAPPY: "The church isn't opposed to this! It's just that I grew up in a church atmosphere, but I never knew what faith in Christ was all about until our church started a systematic program of Bible study. I never understood the Bible, or the meaning of Christ, or any of these things until I quit hiding behind the dishcloths at the bazaars and behind the aprons at the dinners. I feel I've found God—or perhaps he has finally caught up with me!"

MR. WORN-OUT ORGANIZATION MAN: "For too long we have identified church business and church activity with the essence of the Christian faith. . . ."

MR. UNHAPPY: "Hold on—I don't follow you!"

MR. WORN-OUT ORGANIZATION MAN: "Let me put it this way: Is our purpose to become active church-program pushers, or is our purpose to become more effective witnesses and disciples of Christ?"

MR. UNHAPPY: "There's a difference?"

MR. WORN-OUT ORGANIZATION MAN: "What do you think?"

MR. UNHAPPY: "I thought they were a part of the same thing—that the more active and involved people became in the programs and machinery of church organization, the better Christians they were."

MR. WORN-OUT ORGANIZATION MAN: "Then how do
you explain people like Mrs. Happy, who admit they
didn't know anything about the Christian faith until
they got away from some of the programs and time-
consuming activities?"

MR. UNHAPPY: "I still think Pastor Herkimer is all wet.
He's taking this faith business so seriously that all the
fun is gone!"

It is interesting to note that no victory was won—the
final statement by Mr. Unhappy was a self-protective
statement, "*I still think . . . ,*" with a parting salvo at the
pastor, whom he holds responsible. Tact is of vital importance here, because Mr. Unhappy needs to be loved
into a different outlook—not threatened.

The verbal witness at its best employs several basic
foundation stones; without these basic qualities, the words
cannot possibly convey genuine meaning.

1. *Be yourself.* This is so basic that we should probably consider it the most important foundation stone.

2. *Be honest.* Don't be afraid to admit a lack of knowledge; never fear to say, "I don't know."

3. *Be clear in purpose.* Your goal is not to win a debate
or to claim a victory. Your purpose is to get people to think
about things they've never thought about before.

4. *Be alert.* Know when to talk and when to be silent.
Be on guard lest you monopolize the conversation. If the
burden of proof is always being put back on to you, then
be assured somebody is leading you and will never be satisfied with your answers.

5. *Beware of language.* Always use language familiar
to you and the person with whom you are speaking.

6. *Be dependent.* The Holy Spirit of God's presence
will strengthen and guide you.

7. *Be in prayer.* "This spiritual love will speak to
Christ about a brother more than to a brother about
Christ." (Dietrich Bonhoeffer.)

VIII

The Psychological Moment
and the Point of Contact

For everything there is a season, and a time for
every matter under heaven.—Eccl. 3:1.

TIMING IS VERY IMPORTANT: there is a time when joking is proper. There is a time when joking is out of place!
There is a time when serious discussion is vital. There is a
time when it has no place. As a matter of fact, the sensitive person constantly will be aware of both the feelings
of others and the context in which he finds himself. He
is aware that, even for good things, there is a right time
and a wrong time. No one has spoken more aptly of this
fact than the ancient Preacher who said, there is:

a time to be born, and a time to die;
a time to plant, and a time to pluck up what is planted;
a time to kill, and a time to heal;
a time to break down, and a time to build up;
a time to weep, and a time to laugh;
a time to mourn, and a time to dance;
a time to cast away stones, and a time to gather stones
   together;
a time to embrace, and a time to refrain from embracing;
a time to seek, and a time to lose;
a time to keep, and a time to cast away;
a time to rend, and a time to sew;
a time to keep silence, and a time to speak;

a time to love, and a time to hate;
a time for war, and a time for peace.

(Eccl. 3:2–9.)

Just as God prepared the world for the (Incarnation) entry of Jesus, we must do some preparation in the matter of Christian witness. Just to speak the words is not enough! There is such a thing as the right word spoken at the right time in the right way. Too often we forget the matter of timing. We have all noticed that the factor which often spells the difference between a first-line comedian and an also-ran is the matter of timing on jokes. Without a sense of timing, all humor is lost. One cannot help noticing the importance of timing in the space-flight program. The reentry and recovery procedure depends upon exact timing in the firing of retro-rockets. In one U.S. space flight, an error of three seconds caused a "splash down" 250 miles beyond target.

The problem of timing in our witness we shall call the psychological moment. There is a time when certain remarks will be more readily received than at other times. There is a time to speak and a time to be silent. There is a time to listen and there is a time to protest, even vigorously.

Here again, as Christians we must study how best to talk with each person we meet. Not only must we study how best to talk, but how best to deal with a certain person or group; how best to relate or communicate. All witness is lost if it is not well timed! There is a time for me to mention my church; there is a time for me to refrain from mentioning it. There is a time for me to mention my relationship to Christ; there is a time for me to refrain from mentioning it. There is a time for sympathy; there is also a time when too much sympathy can do harm.

The "psychological moment" has to do with sensing when the time is ripe to say or do a certain thing. In each individual case there is no easily determined right and wrong, but only a better and a best. The only way to improvement is through practice and self-analysis of one's method of operation. If we do not work for self-improvement, we shall never feel free and easy in the process of witnessing.

The psychological moment is almost always determined by circumstances surrounding the object of your concern. Death, grief, illness, surgery, disappointment, tragedy, failure, lonesomeness, despondency, depression, discouraging news, worrisome news, as well as times of success, happiness, good news, promotion, birth, family reunion, are all occasions of ministry and witness. In each and every case there is a point in the interpersonal relationship when words spoken can be more effective if they are spoken at the proper time.

The psychological moment is, therefore, that one moment when words spoken can convey real interpersonal meaning, and if spoken at a less opportune time, will be void of help and strength. We learn, as we practice our speaking witness, that there is a precise moment to speak and a precise moment to keep still. There is a time when our words should be short and to the point—not dragging or dwelling on irrelevancies to the present situation.

A young man who had lost his father once asked, "Why does no one look me in the face and simply say, 'I'm sorry'?" This young man discovered that at such a time, people take refuge in wordiness and gabbiness, saying: "I remember how it was when my mother died. . . . I wasn't able to eat for weeks!"

Numerous instances of such superfluous wordiness can be brought to mind by the reader: times of family crisis, hospital visits, funerals, birth-out-of-wedlock, etc. The fault is not so much the lack of compassion by well-meaning people as it is that none of the remarks really come to terms with either the pathos or the meaning of the event. A theology professor once warned his students against the ever-present danger of speaking pious platitudes to people in need. "Everything will be all right!" "Just keep busy and try not to think about it." "It's God's will!"

Lest we become convinced that this psychological moment has to do only with tragedy, pain, sorrow, or death, let us explore further examples drawn from ordinary everyday occurrences. A neighboring housewife comes to your house ostensibly to borrow some sugar. All too often it isn't the sugar she wants, but a sympathetic ear. At this point, you see that you are involved whether you like it or not. Should you give advice? Should you tell her what you would do? Should you condone her every statement? Should you judge her and point out her faults? Here we have a typical incident requiring thought and discretion for the Christian! Better to listen (if time permits at that moment) carefully and to try to discern the real problem, and then thoughtfully and slowly phrase a question that will help the person to gain insight into her own behavior. The psychological moment comes only after one has attentively listened.

The point of contact is part and parcel of the psychological moment, for one deals with encounter and one with the moment of encounter. The point of contact is established only when an opening is created whereby one life may briefly move into verbal and emotional contact with another life. Here we see the uselessness of uttering pious platitudes and trite phrases. It becomes as if a doctor of internal medicine took one look at you on the sidewalk and prescribed a dosage of penicillin. He has prescribed (spoken) without any diagnosis or examination (listening). The encounter has no opportunity of bearing fruit unless there is some relationship established by which and through which words spoken can penetrate in a meaningful way.

The experience of too many people is that when a genuine attempt is made to help them in their predicament or distress, all they get spoken to them is, "The Lord has done this for me!" or "When that happened to me, the Lord did thus and so." Some people are so overtaken by their own so-called "experiences with the Lord" that they feel they must tell everyone they meet of their experience —with no point of contact and with no psychological moment. One is reminded of *The Rime of the Ancient Mariner,* in which a total stranger on his way to a wedding is waylaid by a man seeking someone who would listen to him. Just so, too often we identify Christian witness as this art of capturing a complete stranger, and then overwhelming him with our irrelevant testimony concerning "what the Lord has done for me."

The athletic world provides us with good examples of the psychological moment and the point of contact. In football there is the "delayed block," which is successful only if the timing is perfect. In basketball, football, and baseball there is the psychological moment when the opposition is much more vulnerable than at other moments. This is the time to strike. This is the time to "move in."

A public speaker of almost any variety is concerned with the establishment of a point of contact with his audience, and then he carefully calculates his message so that at the desirable moment he can drive his point home.

What we are speaking of in this chapter is related to what we often hear referred to as the "sixth sense." Jesus' words apply to us: "Do you not yet perceive or understand? Are your hearts hardened? Having eyes do you not see, and having ears do you not hear?" (Mark 8:17–18). There is no easy way to cultivate this sense of perception. We need to work at it; we need to be on guard; we need to practice the habit of alertness. When two lives meet, however unplanned or brief the duration of meeting, there often occurs one fleeting opportunity to communicate in depth. How we use this one opportunity depends upon our ability to size up the situation.

Through the process of asking questions in casual conversation we proceed to establish a dialogue, involving careful speaking and attentive listening. Rarely does it happen that there is no point of contact or psychological moment.

Much of our witness as Christian individuals should follow this pattern; every opportunity requires cultivation and attentive listening. Every encounter should respect the individual—not as a thing to be converted, but as a person standing in the love of Christ whether he knows it or not. Before anything constructive takes place, there must be real personal contact—the point of need, the opening, the eye of the storm! And then the right moment to say carefully what one has on his heart and mind.

A word of caution needs to be spoken. Rarely, if ever, are immediate results either forthcoming or observable. Jesus gave us the parable of the soils (Matt. 13:3–9, 18–23), which illustrates for us that unless the soil is receptive, our planting of seed will go by the boards. Just so, this does not excuse us from the challenge laid upon us by Christ when he said, "You shall be my witnesses," but rather, this parable serves to make us realize that it is not we, but the Holy Spirit of God using us to bring about God's eternal purposes. Some of our seed will fall on rocky places, some on hard earth, some in weeds; but by the grace of God, some will fall on good soil, and it will bear fruit. When that happens, the miracle of witness has unfolded before you.

IX

Witness as Reaction
to the Realities of Life

Paul's witness from prison, "I want you to know, brethren, that what has happened to me has really served to advance the gospel, so that it has become known throughout the whole praetorian guard and to all the rest that my imprisonment is for Christ; and most of the brethren have been made confident in the Lord because of my imprisonment, and are much more bold to speak the word of God without fear." (Phil. 1:12–14.)

A HUMAN LIFE lived in total isolation is not life as God intended life to be. Far more than we dare imagine, our lives are the sum total of thousands upon thousands of little incidents playing upon us, influencing us for better or for worse, molding us, prejudicing us, trying us, judging us, and challenging us. The vast area of interpersonal relationships is still the meat (or pith) of life. Life lived in relation to other lives is the backdrop for the daily living of the Christian faith. Life and time are inseparable, and tragedy ensues when life is wasted and squandered. The greatest waste known in the world today is the waste of a human life.

The Christian faith does not escape life, but claims authority only as an individual faces life in Christ and through Christ. The faith handed down to us for twenty centuries is not an insurance policy against the hard realities and experiences of life; rather, it is the frame-work through which we find our bearings to cope with both the expected and the unexpected. And if we define our "witness" as Christians as the daily living of our faith, then we come to see that our witness is but the totality of our faith at work.

If we could choose the things that were to happen to us in life, we could write a different kind of book: "How to Choose the Realities You Wish to Face in Life in Five Easy Steps." But so much of human experience is not of our own choosing; we did not choose to be born, nor is it our right to choose when we shall die. We choose our husband or our wife, not knowing what the future holds. We choose to bring children into the world, not knowing what joys and sorrows will accompany their arrival and growth.

Who of us would choose cancer, or coronary disease, or arthritis? Who of us would choose war and hatred and misery? Who of us would choose death or handicaps or heartbreak? Who would choose retardation or blindness or ugliness?

Christ himself was faced with this same life and with the opposition and craftiness of those who sought his demise. He did not choose to die, but he chose to be obedient to his Father's will. In Gethsemane he struggled in prayer, in the wilderness he struggled with the temptations to take shortcuts and to compromise his own beliefs. Yet the meaning of the incarnation is precisely that Christ battles life on our terms, because he takes upon himself our limitations (see Phil. 2:5–8).

It is at this point, and only at this point, that the Christian faith seeks to answer the riddles and problems of human life. Our focus is Christ, our perspective is Christ, our example is Christ, our strength is Christ, and our faith is Christ. It is well said that although we do not know what the future holds, we do know *who* holds our future.

What does all this about Christ have to do with our witness? How do we react to birth, death, disease, heartbreak, tragedy, broken homes, infidelity, poverty, unemployment, disillusionment, physical and emotional handicaps, and unhappiness? Do we take what life brings lying down? Do we philosophize to one another as Job's three friends did to him? Do we run away? Do we withdraw into our turtle shells, hoping life will pass us by? Do we become bitter? Do we create a split personality, laughing on the outside and crying on the inside? Do we curse God? Do we defy God or try to bargain with God?

One cannot witness in a vacuum, nor can one witness to a straw dummy! By the grace of God, we are what we are! God knows our plight specifically, because through Christ he experienced this life. Our witness therefore is developed as we face these decisions, dilemmas, and hardships of life. Dietrich Bonhoeffer found himself in prison, and it was from prison that he gave our world the most indelible Christian witness of the modern age. Through Christ and in Christ, he faced his inward doubts, his appetites, his misgivings, his joys, his longings. His witness was in what he said, in what he wrote (his letters to parents and friends), his attitudes toward his captors and fellow prisoners, and in his living in the daily strength of Christ where he was (in prison) doing what he had to do at that moment (remaining in captivity).

One of the most striking examples of witness as reaction to the realities of life is to be found in the book by Ernest Gordon, *Through the Valley of the Kwai*. Out of suffering, disease, atrocity, and filth, came the experience of new life. Dr. Gordon describes in penetrating terms the coming of the Holy Spirit and the reality of the koinonia. "Ours was the church of the spirit. It was the throbbing heart which gave life to the camp and transformed it in considerable measure from a mass of frightened individuals into a community. From it we received the inspiration that made life possible. Such inspiration was not merely a rosy glow in the abdomen, but the literal in-breathing of the Holy Spirit that enabled men to live nobler lives, to become kind neighbors, to create improvements for the good of others, including such mundane matters as learning to cook better rice. The fruits of the Holy Spirit were clearly in evidence—'love, joy, long-suffering, gentleness, peace, goodness and faith.' " The faith of two or three men eventually spread throughout the entire prison camp. Their vital witness influenced others and a chain reaction resulted.

One of the foremost intellectual stumbling blocks to acceptance of the Christian faith is the problem of evil and suffering. Yet it is the testimony of countless thousands of Christians that it was at just such a time of great personal crisis that they first came to a vital, meaningful faith in God. Reaction to crisis is usually not an immediate victory of faith. More often faith that is real has been hammered out on the anvil of suffering and doubt, despair and deep soul-searching. Yet the witness that comes out of these experiences is often far more penetrating than any other kind of witness imaginable.

A young woman came home from the hospital in order to spend her last days in her own bed. She had terminal cancer. Neighbors who visited her and friends who wanted to help her discovered that she was the one who had helped them. She was not a pious religionist, but she was a servant of Jesus Christ. She believed his plain words, "When I go and prepare a place for you, I will come again and will take you to myself, that where I am you may be also" (John 14:3). She told people that she had nothing to fear and *that she was glad she knew about her condition.* Her attitude and reaction to the immediate prospect of death influenced scores of people. When death came, it appeared as though her own faith had infiltrated the minds and hearts of her husband and children. Their witness was a powerful force in that neighborhood.

When Paul said, "I can do all things in him who strengthens me" (Phil. 4:13), he was speaking from concrete personal experience, as one having been debased, derided, imprisoned. He had faced poverty and abundance, he had received the strength of Christ to face the hard knocks of life, and now his witness was in sharing this with others.

Our reaction to the realities of life prepares us to be witnesses in two ways. First, our reaction to what happens to us is a very vital part of our witness. But beyond the immediate time, place, and circumstances of our reaction, there is another important kind of witness that can be defined as our witness to others as they take their turn at facing the realities of life. Perhaps our difficulties and sufferings have long since become ancient personal history; nevertheless, we are now better qualified to witness and minister to others because of the fact that *we have been where they now are*. We can identify; we have a better opportunity to establish a good rapport because of the fact that we too bear the mark of suffering and pain.

The thing that makes a man's witness powerful and meaningful is the fact that this is how his faith has operated in his own life. When a Christian tells this story in love, in genuine regard for the other person, and in the prayer that the Holy Spirit will use his witness, great things can happen. The layman who is sensitive to what has happened to a person can oftentimes be far more helpful in his witness than can any clergyman. His remarks are his; they are completely sincere; they are original and (hopefully) not polished or refined. The contention of this entire book is that this witness by the layman is precisely what we mean when we talk about the mutual ministry of all Christians.

Your life and your attitude toward life (what you believe) give you a background from which to minister to your fellowman. You have experienced joy and sorrow, love and disappointment, heartache and grief; you have had close calls, narrow escapes, and utterly real temptations; you have put your trust in a friend and have been let down by him; you have been betrayed or crossed by one you thought you could trust implicitly; you have lived with your desires, your drives, your failings, and your weaknesses. You are unique: you have a faith and you have a message to share. You share it at the point of contact and at the psychological moment, but what you share has been brewing and taking shape for years as you yourself have faced the realities of life. Pious religious talk is frivolous and unnecessary; yet who is so shallow and narrow that they would define witness as "pious talk"? All that is asked of you is personal testimony—it may sound "religious" or it may not—which enables you to identify with a person with whom at this moment you find yourself in contact and in relationship.

Your witness combines silence, words, gestures, facial expressions, nods, and an undefinable attribute of genuine concern that speaks louder and more clearly than a thousand theological lectures. That this witness may require personal sacrifice is obvious. It will cost you time and energy; it may cost you peace of mind and not a few worrisome and sleepless nights. It may cost you certain family plans or cherished activities: all of this in the name and for the sake of Jesus Christ, to whom you have committed yourself. Therefore, to bear witness is to *be* something, not just to *say* or *do* something. It is to be a disciple working, sharing, living as one who has given his life as a servant to his master.

X

Witness in the Use of Time, Talents, and Money

> The life of stewardship is nothing less than "total devotion" to the Christ who is known as a "real, living personal presence in the hearts of believers," a genuine loyalty that is expressed not in mere opinion or sentiment but in character and conduct.—T. A. Kantonen.

A STEWARD is one who has been entrusted with something to use, to control, and to govern its use. Jesus talks about stewards, "Who then is the faithful and wise steward, whom his master will set over his household?" (Luke 12:42.) "And he called him and said to him, 'What is this that I hear about you? Turn in the account of your stewardship, for you can no longer be steward.'" (Luke 16:2.) Also, Peter uses the word "steward" in I Peter 4:10, and Paul in Titus 1:7 and in I Cor. 4:1. A steward is a trustee with whom has been lodged certain responsibilities.

The thesis of this chapter is that as Christ's witnesses, we are also his stewards. God has entrusted us with certain gifts. These gifts are not ours to abuse but to use. These gifts are given to enjoy, but not to squander; to develop, but not to waste. Life itself is the most precious of these gifts. In addition we list our loved ones, family, friends, health, strength, and our mental ability. The writer of I Peter says, "As each has received a gift, employ it for one another, as good stewards of God's varied grace:

whoever speaks, as one who utters oracles of God; whoever renders service, as one who renders it by the strength which God supplies; in order that in everything God may be glorified through Jesus Christ." (I Peter 4:10–11a.)

TIME

Our stewardship of time is very revealing. As witnesses, ministers, and ambassadors of Christ, we are entrusted with precious moments. Many theologians and philosophers have contended that one of the most pressing problems facing twentieth-century America is the problem of what to do with leisure time. By leisure time we mean time left over between required sleep and required work.

The problem of leisure is the problem of what to do with our time. Do we watch TV? Do we have hobbies? Do we exercise? Do we putter around the house in do-it-yourself projects? Do we read? Do we serve the community through some volunteer agency? Do we sleep?

QUESTION: What's wrong with those things? I like to watch TV, play golf, read, water-ski, and when there's no way out, I give in to my wife and do the chores around the house!

ANSWER: There's nothing wrong with these things, as long as they are done in moderation and with purpose. The idea of the golden mean of the ancient Greek philosophers is still to be taken seriously. Jesus was not an ascetic like John the Baptist. Jesus was not an abstainer. The point to be made is that a well-balanced life allows time for many varied pursuits and interests; as stewards of the gift of time, we are to fill this time wholesomely.

Show me a person who never reads, and I will show you a narrow mind. Show me a person who doesn't take proper exercise and healthy recreation, and I will show you a person who abuses the temple of God's Holy Spirit. Show me a person who does nothing but sit in front of the "one-eyed monster" and I will show you a man who has gone stale. Part of our witness that we make constantly to those around us is this usage of our leisure time. We tell others what we believe by how we spend our time. We show forth our personal code of values by the way we organize our lives, our years, our months, our weeks, our days, our hours, and even our minutes.

Time is precious! It is a gift. Moments gone by are moments never to be repeated. The Christian senses this, and he senses that he has been given this time to use, not to squander. Some of it is to be used on oneself, and some should be spent in behalf of others. Some should involve concentration, and some should be completely relaxing.

We show by what we do with our leisure time how seriously we take to heart the Christian gospel. Although I can think of nothing that more resembles a stuffed shirt than a theologian who studies *all* day long, I can think of nothing more wasteful than for a man to be sleeping or playing golf in *all* his leisure hours.

Time is something we don't own! We experience it and we use it. We invest it. A Christian witness seeks for balance and moderation; he seeks to be of service to worthwhile organizations and community projects. He seeks to read, to keep himself adequately informed concerning daily events in God's world and in the affairs of men and nations. He seeks to enrich himself with the wisdom of the past and with the best writing of the present. He seeks to be a father, a husband, a son. The Christian has no part of fun that comes at another's expense or that degrades human life. The Christian looks for opportunity to serve and opportunity to minister. He engages in his own ministry of personal helpfulness. He seeks to give meaning and purpose to every leisure moment he has.

The Christian witness budgets his time so that he does not spread himself too thin. He is diligent in his primary responsibilities to his vocation, to his family, and to his church. He is not a Johnny-one-note, nor is he a social gadfly. He sees his life as a gift from God, entrusted to his own use for a brief span of time. He realizes the transiency of time, and he therefore has a perspective of urgency in the things he undertakes. He senses that life is very short and can be lived, as we know it, but once. He is therefore selective in his usage of all his leisure.

TALENTS

A second way we must be on guard is in the matter of how we use our capacities and abilities. It is a tragic waste to see the stewardship level of many Christians in this regard.

Whether we are one-talent people or ten-talent people is irrelevant. Stewardship is the way we use that one or that ten. Whether it be playing the piano for a Sunday school department or doing a yearly audit for the board of trustees of one's church, the question is still the same, Are we using our capabilities wisely in His service?

At this point, the church is entirely too self-centered. Our thoughts concerning talent turn immediately to the building at the corner of Main and Spruce Streets, which we call "our church."

But this is not the point. The church today is becoming increasingly aware of its responsibilities to the social order and to the world for which Christ died. Therefore, we dare not think only of using talents and abilities in church work per se. There are Red Cross units, blood-mobiles, auxiliary police, volunteer fire departments, recreational leagues, Boy Scouts, Girl Scouts, old age homes, nursing homes, community chest drives, slum-clearance projects, political party campaigns.

Whether the individual Christian is a doctor or a plumber, a schoolteacher or a factory worker, he insults God when he says to himself: "I am of no account. What good is the little I can do?" This is a slap in God's face! Do you not know that your body is the temple of the Holy Spirit? Do you not realize that you are unique on the face of this earth and that you are created in the image of God? Do you dare despise this person you are by deflating yourself in false humility? When God called Moses, Moses' first reaction was to say, "Oh, my Lord, send, I pray, some other person" (Ex. 4:13). Is this our answer?

There is no doubt that those in the church who constitute its clergy have done a poor job of marshaling the talents and abilities of the people. All too often the church officers enlist people in the army of Christ and then give them nothing to do.

In this regard, the church has more wasted manpower and potential than any other institution on the face of the earth! Nevertheless, the blame cannot be placed entirely on the clergy, for as witnesses of Christ, we need not wait for the church or for the "minister" to get us a job! As His witnesses, we are stewards who possess gifts of many varieties and descriptions. These capabilities and talents are ours to use, not to sit on or to hide under a bushel. We Christians have a job to do, and we have the potential to do it. But we won't do it as long as we believe our own excuses.

A witness is entrusted with the keeping and wise usage of his talents and capabilities as surely as he is entrusted with the usage of his time. Here is a field for creative imagination and for thorough study: the church has failed to mobilize its manpower; yet we are the church. We are His body because we are his witnesses. We have a job to do: part of our witness is the willingness to use our abilities and talents, meager as we think they are, in the doing of this job.

MONEY

The third major area of stewardship is the one many people associate completely as being the sum and substance of the meaning of the word: i.e., money. The getting and spending of money occupies the greater portion of our waking hours. As witnesses for Jesus Christ, we cannot be laggards in giving money to the church.

There is no such thing as a self-made man! No man

upon the face of the earth can take exclusive credit for his achievement of financial wealth. We work, but God gives us our every breath! We work, but God sustains us and gives us the mental and physical resources we need.

As his witnesses we are called to share this livelihood, not with token payments or with tips, but with the first-fruits of our labor. Percentage-giving of one's income, whether it be 10 percent, 20 percent, or 30 percent, is a matter of faith and commitment to Christ himself. I have never known a committed person to begrudge his church pledge. People who are not interested in taking Christ seriously will, of course, always be around to protest that "all the church wants is my money." As Christ's disciples and witnesses we should be appalled at the many gimmicks many churches use to raise funds. The church in which people see themselves as Christ's witnesses, and therefore mean business in turning their daily lives completely over to his rulership and direction, has no problem meeting a budget.

We Christians who talk about witnessing and about giving our lives to Christ had better take a good, long, hard look at our financial stewardship habits. This is not to insist on the tithe, but it is to insist on an honest soul-searching evaluation of our individual financial giving and spending. It is a myth to tell ourselves that giving shouldn't hurt or that it should not entail any sacrifice. Our modern culture has emptied the meaning of the word "sacrifice," and we modern Christians in the United States have little, if any, concept of real Christlike sacrifice.

Let it be said clearly that not all of one's giving need be to the local church. But, let it be said even more clearly, that until we Christian witnesses begin to understand the meaning of discipline in our commitment to Christ, everything else we do and say is mere habit and ritual. Christians today talk a better game than they play. Christians today agree intellectually with much of what the church says, but they guard their pocketbooks with a passion. We do not give to a need until we are committed to a cause.

In this context we must consider the problem of materialism in our modern culture. The things that money can buy are made attractive to us. We must not be dishonest with ourselves; we cannot pretend that we are not attracted to such things as modern conveniences, luxuries, homes, labor-saving devices, and fine furniture.

"But what then are we to do? Deny ourselves everything? Surely we are not being called to give Christ all our income!" Comments such as this point up the fact that our prime allegiance is either to God or to ourselves. If we take our weekly paycheck and spend it on necessities, and then if we say, "Well, is this remaining money to be spent for me or for God?" then the battle line has been formed and the decision will be painful; indeed, the chances are that God will come out second best. This is why Christ is to be represented at the top of our budget, and never at the bottom. What portion we give to God sanctifies the portion we retain for our own necessities.

God	Taxes
Food	Car
Clothing	Household
Mortgage or Rent	Savings
Utilities	Entertainment
Insurance	Recreation
Medical	Extras

The discipline involved is the discipline of priorities. When Christ comes first, the amount seems to fall into place. When Christ comes first, the money to be used for the family will be used with greater discretion and with less foolishness. Therefore, the stewardship of money is a two-sided affair: How much do we share with Christ? How well do we use the remainder for our own needs?

XI

The Christian Witness
Takes a Stand

> The Christian life is a commitment to Christ
> and a compulsion to witness. . . . In our Hebrew-
> Christian heritage the man of faith is the passion-
> ate man. . . . His life is totally wagered against
> overwhelming odds that God is and that He cares
> to redeem. . . . It is an exhilarating abandonment
> of security. It is a moving out into life. It is the
> insanity of believing God. It is flinging oneself
> into grandeur. It is possession by the One who still
> creates. Commitment requires unbelievable cour-
> age. To the Christian it is betting everything that
> the Galilean was not a fraud, but a Savior.—
> Robert C. Strom.

Until now, we have confined our discussion of witness
to the ordinary realm of daily existence and daily decision.
There comes a time, however, when as His witnesses, we
must take some official stand on a pressing social issue or
community crisis. At such a time the behavior, attitude,
and remarks of the Christian are of vital importance, both
in what they contribute to effective resolution of the problem and in what they may fail to do.

No one likes a coward, and yet the alternative to cowardice need not be headstrong, impulsive, irresponsible
behavior. To the conscientious and sensitive Christian,
neither cowardice nor bandwagon shouting are acceptable
alternatives.

Sometimes the stand we take concerns the abuses, symptoms, and dangers of alcohol. Sometimes it may be right-to-work laws or issues resulting in union-management disputes. It could be the race question, civil rights, politics, or local zoning laws. It could be the situation wherein a local school district is putting undue pressure on its local high school coach to "be a winner or else!" The issue could be over taxes, over local ordinances, over the conduct of the P.T.A., or over administration of the local Boy Scout troop.

When a Christian takes a stand, he may find himself in the public eye or in a very private conference room. He may be utterly and completely alone, or he may have lots of support. He may discover that it is indeed important to have the right kind of enemies in life. A man is not only known by the friends and company he keeps, but by those who oppose him. Christ had enemies; he was constantly involved in controversy and faced with unfriendly agitators.

The only ways the individual follower of Christ can avoid these issues and modern dilemmas are: (1) by seeking escape from life by entering the monastery or retreat house (to run away, to seek refuge in solitude); (2) by simply shutting his eyes to the problems of humanity and seeking inner solace and peace by constantly reminding himself, "It isn't really my concern," and "What good would it do if I did get involved?" Neither of these possibilities is a satisfactory answer for the Christian. The only real option that is open to us is that of facing the issue honestly and squarely. Sound thinking must be done!

The question of taking a stand is one of considerable difference in opinion even among Christians. For instance, a teen-ager is faced with the problem of drinking. Solution No. 1 might be very easy: there is no problem because Christians don't drink! Solution No. 2: drink. Solution No. 3: drink moderately. Solution No. 4: abstain graciously. Solution No. 5: abstain self-righteously

and obnoxiously. With clear conscience, any of these five
have been offered as answers to the teen-ager as being
"Christian" solutions to the problem. The question I
would ask is, Is there a polite way for the teen-ager to say
no and yet maintain his rapport and respect among his
peers?

Here are two teetotalers who both feel the same way
about alcohol: one is a pompous, self-righteous snob who
makes everybody in his presence feel ill; the other is a
gentle soul with a fabulous sense of humor. Is it necessary to predict which one will make the most effective
stand and influence the most people toward his point of
view? How blessed we are when we can laugh at our own
beliefs! (Why must we Christians be stuffed shirts? Have
we lost the blessing of a sense of humor?)

Perhaps the most difficult area of conduct is in determining if I, as a witness of Christ, am to be a middle-
of-the-roader, a fence-sitter, or a person of action and
commitment! This is not an easy question; for in some
situations I may feel compelled to speech and action, but
in other instances I may honestly be in a mental dilemma
as to what I really think and how I really feel.

We can look at some of the racial dilemmas of the past
decade to illustrate this problem. When should a Christian
get into the act? When should a Christian be a part of a
demonstration? When should a Christian permit himself
to be jailed? On the other hand, many sensitive Christians
refuse to be a part of mass demonstrations. It is a good
question: Am I abstaining from mass demonstrations because I basically don't want to be involved in controversy,
or because I honestly don't think it's the answer? And
then we ask, Did I arrive at my answer via rationalization
to defend and justify my subconscious desire to be free
of the whole situation?

Whether we are discussing the question of living next
door to a Negro or the question of the Negro's contribu-

tion to his own cause, the Christian still is called upon for his opinion and, if need be, his stand.

It is not too much to say that we Christians are often judged by the way we stand up for the ideals to which we give lip service. The world needs our leadership: the great issues of our day need our best thinking and our best constructive criticism. Although it is obvious that Christians do not present a united front on matters of social concern, nevertheless this fact does not justify our shirking away from declaring ourselves and acting prudently upon our declaration.

Perhaps we all need to be reminded that silence is a form of consent, and that through the silence of Christian witnesses many an important cause has been lost. If Mr. Hesitation can't make up his mind to get on the train now waiting in the terminal, his mind will soon be made up for him by the engineer, who will pull the throttle in exactly thirty seconds. If Mr. Hesitation still can't decide, he will be left on the platform as the train pulls out. *Not to decide is to decide.* Just so, it is not our right to sit on the sidelines as Christ's soldiers, cheering the participants onward to victory. We are not spectators! As followers of Christ, we are involved whether we choose to be or not.

To those who protest that they do not approve of the type of stands some people take, it needs to be pointed out clearly that this is their right, but having said it does not excuse them from seeking out a constructive and creative way of taking their own stand and making their own witness. Christians today cannot afford the illusory luxury of noncommitment.

It is not uncommon today to hear parents bemoan the fact that their children and teen-agers want to go along with the crowd; they are afraid to be different, afraid of losing their group status, afraid of being ostracized, or of being called a square. Is it not the adult generation that has posted the way so well for this attitude?

One parent is afraid of what might happen if she insists that her daughter be in the house by one A.M., after a dance, instead of three A.M. Another parent is concerned that if his son doesn't go with the crowd that drinks beer, he will be emotionally retarded and crippled for life.

We need not be great or renowned in order to make a constructive contribution by taking our stand. The rank and file of Christian witnesses will not have their names in the newspapers until their golden wedding anniversary, or until their obituary appears. Nevertheless, these are the soldiers of the cross who win the battles, who change the tide, who overpower the forces of evil. These are the people who will bring equal human rights for the Negro, who will ensure the dignity of human life, who will dethrone corrupt governments, who will overpower apathetic public officials, who will keep a nonchampionship football coach from being fired, who will prevent labor union dictatorships, who will not be bullied into following the crowd or into blind acceptance of the *status quo*.

We cannot deny that a Christian's stand, even though it be done with sincerity and with a thoroughgoing assessment of all possible ramifications and results, will at times cost him. It is about time we realized that Christ died for us, and the thing he asks of us in return is our lives! Yes, it will cost us! It may cost us our pride, our job, our popularity, our community "image"; it may cost us the closeness of family ties (as when parents can't believe their twenty-five-year-old child would embarrass them by taking a public stand against a new zoning law), or the closeness of friends who may think we've become fanatics or "gone overboard"; it may cost us a few nights' sleep, or a few months' sleep; it may cost us our peace of mind and our family's well-being. We have no right to expect that we won't have to pay a price. This business of being a Christian is not all peaches and cream. Sometimes we need to be rudely awakened to the filth of life, to the gutters, the graft, the animallike sex ethics, the cheapness of life. This is not to imply that life is not also good and lovely and wonderful. It is. But if we follow Christ long enough and far enough, he will lead us down these uncomfortable paths. (See Luke 14:25–35; see also Matt. 10:37 for insight into Luke 14:26.)

And so the stand we Christians are called upon to take is as varied and different as are the myriads of circumstances surrounding the individual situation. There are no laws and no rules. However, some practical guidelines can be summarized:

1. Pray your way through difficult issues and decisions.

2. Act wisely and judiciously. Keep an open mind; seek out all the facts on all sides of the question.

3. Don't lead with your emotions: let your emotional feeling follow your wise judgment.

4. Sit where others sit: try on the other fellow's shoes and walk around in them for at least a day.

5. Love your enemies or your adversary. Without the love of Christ to control us we are helpless. (See I Cor., ch. 13.)

6. Be prepared to pay the cost.

7. Do not be arrogant or flippant. Do not be cowardly; let your stand and your strength reinforce others.

8. Constantly reexamine your own position. Seek to fortify it.

9. Don't be afraid of failure or of being a minority. Minorities can be powerful. Failure sometimes comes to us as it did to Christ.

10. Don't be pressured or bullied into action for action's sake! Don't be too quick to endorse every new wind of doctrine that blows. Keep your head, even when others appear to be losing theirs. (See Eph. 4:14.)

11. Read and reread the four Gospels. Notice how Christ handled himself amid the controversies of his time.

XII

Preparation for Witness

This is the meaning of "grace." It was in the cross that the grace of God appeared and was unveiled in history, as his purpose and our hope. "Grace" is another word for "love," except that it carries the additional meaning that the love is totally *unmerited,* completely *unearned,* and absolutely *undeserved.* It can be called "in-spite-of" love, because it is offered and given *in spite of* the fact that its recipient in no way deserves to be loved with this kind of love.—Robert Clyde Johnson.

THE CHRISTIAN FAITH is full of paradox. In dying, we are raised from the dead. In seeking God's Kingdom first, we have all else added unto us. In giving ourselves to Christ, we find ourselves. In confession, we experience the meaning of forgiveness.

Many people seek to define their faith by saying that they accept Jesus as a great teacher and spiritual leader. According to this view, it is Jesus' teachings that contain the sum and substance of Christianity. But when we take Christ's call seriously, we find that he calls us, not just to his teachings, but to himself utterly and completely. We discover that he calls us to be his, not just spiritually, but mentally, socially, physically, emotionally, morally, and materially. He doesn't ask just our admiration; he asks our life in response to his sacrifice for us. And therefore when we seek to follow him long enough and far enough, we discover that he leads us not only into the koinonia of his body but also to share his cross.

The more earnestly we desire to obey him, the more clearly we see how utterly we fail him. The more we seek to be faithful to him, the more keenly aware we become of our shortcomings and our sin.

Sin is the opposite of faith, and it consists of anything and everything that in any way separates us from the love of God. The essential character of sin is disobedience, and the result is separation from self, from fellowman, and from God.

It is because of this "separation resulting from sin" that the Christian needs to prepare himself for witness. This preparation consists of confessional prayer and disciplined study of the Scriptures. Although there are many things helpful in preparation, these are basic. Study leads to knowledge and understanding of the entire Christian message. Confession leads to forgiveness and the experience of grace.

CONFESSION AND FORGIVENESS

Only as we comprehend the radical nature of sin can we begin to understand the meaning of forgiveness. Forgiveness makes life possible. Forgiveness releases us from the guilt of past sin. Forgiveness is not license. "If God will forgive and forgive and forgive, why should I bother to live a 'good' life? Why not eat, drink, and be merry, for God always forgives?" This is a question of intellect rather than emotion. When a person really experiences and comprehends in depth the meaning of God's forgiveness, he seeks to respond to it—not by deliberately having a spree-for-all, but by seeking to be a worthy recipient of all that has been done for him and given to him. (See Paul's treatment of this in Rom., chs. 5; 6.)

The individual Christian is a witness for Christ. We point others to Him or away from Him by all we do and say. And yet, who are we to do this? Who are we to tell others? Who do I think I am? Is this whole thing not simply an exercise in scandalous, pompous audacity?

This is why, as witnesses, we need confessional prayer. We are not to be "pious" or "religious" or "pompous" or "presumptuous." But we are to live by the grace we proclaim. If we are to do this, we need to keep our lives in constant communication with God. This is done through prayer. And the beginning of prayer is when we bare ourselves before him who is God and Lord, Judge and Redeemer. We lay our life in his hands. We strip away our false fronts of smiling, successful Americans, and cry out to God "out of the depths" (Ps. 130:1). We rid ourselves of the facade that we cleverly and subconsciously use to protect ourselves. We ask God to renew us, to have mercy upon us, to make us into new creatures.

In confession we fight through our unworthy desires, our honest reservations, our limited commitment, our foolish decisions, our hasty remarks, our silence when we should have spoken. With Paul we confess that we do not understand our own actions: at times we do not do the good we want to do, and at other times we do the very thing we do not want to do (read Rom. 7:13–25). In confession we unlock the door of our innermost souls. We invite God in for a look; we allow him complete access into all the dim nooks and crannies. The searching brilliance of his eternal light cleanses us, purifies us, and strengthens us to face the world with a clear conscience.

In confession, we do the work; in forgiveness, God acts. We bare our souls; God responds by granting us the miracle of forgiveness. It is important for us to grasp this fact because we need to realize that forgiveness is a concrete act of God. God does something! God acts! God erases! God forgets! God wipes the slate clean! Our only responsibility is to bring ourselves to the state of total repentance. This we do by thoroughgoing confession every day of our lives.

If we protest and say that this last chapter is just a lot of tacked-on theological jargon, then to what is the Christian witness to witness? How can we witness to the unmerited loving grace of God if we have never experienced this grace? How can we give witness to something we have not experienced? How can we witness to the way of Christ if we fail to accept the first step in following Christ, which is to give him our lives so completely that he makes us into new creatures? How can we witness to the faith of Christ if we ourselves do not daily replenish our bodies and souls on the water and bread that Christ gives (see John 6:35)?

As Christians we are called to be his witnesses. And yet, how often we fail Christ before we get started because we don't put first things first. If a witness of Christ has one primary responsibility that takes precedence over all other pressing responsibilities, it is this need to live by confesson. There is no other way for a soldier of the cross to prepare himself for the battle.

STUDY AND COMMITMENT

All that has been said in the foregoing pages is written with one basic assumption in the author's mind. Although this assumption, or this premise, is to this point unspoken, it is the one necessary ingredient upon which all Christian witness is built. *To be a witness of Jesus Christ, one must know something about Christ.* How else can one point to Christ? What is the "content" of our witness? It is Jesus Christ, Lord and Savior.

Therefore, all witness begins with our own intimate knowledge of Jesus Christ as our personal Lord. This knowledge must be of two kinds: it must include an academic knowledge of the Biblical drama of salvation as well as a personal experience-oriented knowledge of Jesus Christ. A teen-age girl may have a crush on the boy who moves in next door. She inquires about this boy and discovers his age, his name, his hobbies, his class schedule, his interests. She knows all *about* him, but as yet she *has not been introduced to him.* It is the same way with our knowledge of Christ and of the Christian faith. We can have a firm grasp on the basic academic issues without ever having met Jesus Christ as the personal Lord of our daily life. Without this personal knowledge of Christ, one has no content and no basis for his witness! How can we witness about him whom we do not know? As Tom Allan writes in his book *The Face of My Parish:* "It is supremely important that any man who is expected to bear a Christian witness should know beyond any shadow of a peradventure where he stands now. He should be a man for whom penitence and faith are not merely theological terms, *but an expression of his own experience of God. No distinctive Christian witness is possible without it.*" (Italics mine.)

It is one thing to believe a set of academic propositions *about* Jesus Christ; it is something else to believe *in* Jesus Christ to the point where we are willing to entrust our lives unto his direction and care. A Christian witness should seek to have *both* kinds of knowledge: this is the foundation upon which our witness is built.

Disciplined study is not an option; it is a basic requirement. How else are we to be familiar with the Christian message that we are to proclaim? The Scriptures, especially the Gospels, The Acts, and the letters of Paul, are a great help in providing us with the content of our witness. The Scriptures are our primary source of testimony concerning Jesus Christ: how can we know about Christ without the eyewitness accounts of the early Christians?

It is the teaching function of the church to provide Christians with the opportunity to study. Our study may be of many varieties and types: discussion, dialogue, lecture, reading groups, workshops. In addition to the Bible, there is a great need for us to study Christian literature especially written for the layman. Beyond this, there is much nontheological and nonreligious literature that we Christians would do well to read, digest, and discuss.

Our study should be done both alone and in small groups. There is no substitute for a faithful daily reading of the Scriptures; there is also no substitute for group discussion where the thinking of others contributes to our own insight and vice versa. Paul's advice to young Timothy applies to us: "Do your best to present yourself to God as one approved, a workman who has no need to be ashamed, rightly handling the word of truth" (II Tim. 2:15).

Study alone can never be a substitute for individual commitment. It is never enough to believe things *about* Jesus Christ, God, and the church! Our personal trust must be *in* Christ as Lord and Savior. Isaiah had a vision of the Lord God. He "heard the voice of the Lord saying, 'Whom shall I send, and who will go for us?' " Isaiah answered, "Here am I! Send me." (Isa. 6:8.) This is the response of the grateful heart. Isaiah was prepared to entrust his future to God. He put his life squarely on the line. Commitment such as this is what Christ expects from those who bear his name. Only as we respond to Christ's call, "Come, follow me," do we gain a personal acquaintance with him.

As we seek to follow in faithful obedience, we experience the firsthand kind of knowledge that no book can provide. A secondhand familiarity will never suffice! Christ seeks to be at home within us in the same way Paul experienced: "I have been crucified with Christ; it is no longer I who live, but Christ who lives in me; and the life I now live in the flesh I live by faith in the Son of God, who loved me and gave himself for me" (Gal.

2:20). It is the discipline of study combined with the discipline of prayer that leads us to commitment to him about whom we study and through whom we pray.

Therefore, we begin where we end, and we end where we begin. As followers of Jesus Christ we must be involved in constant study of the Christian faith. This academic pursuit is completely necessary if we are to be familiar with the Biblical narrative and the history of the Christian church. At the same time, we must submit ourselves to the rigorous discipline of private and corporate prayer, and private and corporate worship. We must seek to equip ourselves with knowledge about Christ, and with personal acquaintance of him as the living Lord of our daily lives. We must know what we believe about him even as we proclaim our trust in him.

A group of anxious Christians were one day eagerly anticipating the "inside scoop" that their Lord would give them now that he had risen from the grave. " 'Lord, will you at this time restore the kingdom to Israel?' He said to them, 'It is not for you to know times or seasons which the Father has fixed by his own authority. But you shall receive power when the Holy Spirit has come upon you; and you shall be my witnesses in Jerusalem and in all Judea and Samaria and to the end of the earth.' " (Acts 1:6–8.)

And so his witnesses we are. Let us be about our task with love, with humility, with vitality, with understanding, and in constant dependence upon the forgiving strength and grace of God. Let us be "wise as serpents and innocent as doves" (Matt. 10:16), always conducting ourselves wisely toward everyone, making the most of every opportunity. Let our speech always be gracious, seasoned with salt, so that we may know how we ought to answer everyone (Col. 4:5–6, paraphrase).

References

IN THIS VOLUME reference is made to the following books, which are listed in the order of their use:

CHAPTER I

Dietrich Bonhoeffer, *The Cost of Discipleship* (The Macmillan Company, 1949), p. 49.

William Barclay, *More New Testament Words* (Harper & Row, Publishers, Inc., 1958), pp. 33–37.

Bonhoeffer, *The Cost of Discipleship*, p. 49.

Ernest Gordon, *Through the Valley of the Kwai* (Harper & Row, Publishers, Inc., 1962), p. 209.

Helmut Thielicke, *The Waiting Father* (Harper & Row, Publishers, Inc., 1959), p. 145.

Francis O. Ayres, *The Ministry of the Laity* (The Westminster Press, 1962), p. 37.

CHAPTER II

Elton Trueblood, *The Company of the Committed* (Harper & Row, Publishers, Inc., 1961), p. 42.

Bonhoeffer, *The Cost of Discipleship*, p. 7.

Robert A. Raines, *New Life in the Church* (Harper & Row, Publishers, Inc., 1961), p. 65.

CHAPTER III

Robert McAfee Brown, *The Bible Speaks to You* (The Westminster Press, 1955), pp. 234–235.

CHAPTER IV

Emil Brunner, *The Divine Imperative* (The Westminster Press, 1947), p. 291.

Howard Clark Kee, *Making Ethical Decisions* (The Westminster Press, 1957), p. 62.

CHAPTER V

Charles W. Forman, *A Faith for the Nations* (The Westminster Press, 1957), p. 89.

John Sutherland Bonnell, *Psychology for Pastor and People* (Harper & Brothers, 1948), p. 55.

Bonhoeffer, *Life Together* (Harper & Brothers, 1954), p. 97.

CHAPTER VI

Trueblood, *The Company of the Committed,* p. 53.

CHAPTER VII

Bonhoeffer, *Life Together,* p. 36.

CHAPTER IX

Bonhoeffer, *Prisoner for God* (The Macmillan Company, 1953).

Gordon, *Through the Valley of the Kwai,* p. 174. Also see Chapters 5, 6, 7.

CHAPTER X

T. A. Kantonen, *A Theology for Christian Stewardship* (Muhlenberg Press, 1956), p. 7.

CHAPTER XI

Robert C. Strom, *Behold a New Thing* (Division of Evangelism, Board of National Missions), p. 39.

CHAPTER XII

Robert Clyde Johnson, *The Meaning of Christ* (The Westminster Press, 1958), p. 48.

Tom Allan, *The Face of My Parish* (Harper & Brothers, 1957), p. 64.